T0361293

ENARRATIO CATULLIANA

CARMINA
L, XXX, LXV, LXVIII

MNEMOSYNE

BIBLIOTHECA CLASSICA BATAVA

COLLEGERUNT

W. DEN BOER, W. J. VERDENIUS, R. E. H. WESTENDORP-BOERMA
BIBLIOTHECAE FASCICULOS
EDENDOS CURAVIT W. J. VERDENIUS, HOMERUSLAAN 53, ZEIST

SUPPLEMENTUM DECIMUM

CHARLES WITKE

ENARRATIO CATULLIANA

CARMINA
L, XXX, LXV, LXVIII

LUGDUNI BATAVORUM E. J. BRILL 1968

ENARRATIO CATULLIANA

CARMINA
L, XXX, LXV, LXVIII

BY

CHARLES WITKE

LEIDEN
E. J. BRILL
1968

PREFACE

Critics of classical literature in the past several decades have embarked upon new readings of old texts with the energy and sincerity of the newly or hastily converted. The results of this "New Criticism" are encountered almost everywhere, in the journals and in books. While it would be futile to pretend that all of these speculative studies are of equal merit, still, few are mere heuristic exercises. One may wonder why another set of essays on a popular author is presented. If these remarks have any point beyond whatever new possibilities they suggest for reading these poems, they teach a distrust for the system of criticism which assumes an importance greater than or distinguished from the poem in question. Any poem is of course unique in special ways; each poem is also like every other poem. If undue stress is given the first proposition here, it is only to redress the balance and redirect critical attention upon the poet's words and the order which they create in a reader's consciousness. If we learn how to read a given text or author, we can learn what questions to ask after reading has ended and criticism has begun. It is instructive to see how many such questions are not only suggested by the poet himself in and through his text but also answered there.

I should like to express my thanks to J. P. Elder, Richard T. Bruère, Joseph Fontenrose, Louis A. MacKay and the University of California, Berkeley, for facilitating this study. It is regrettable that the publication of this work has been delayed some two years after it was accepted by this Series; several important studies have appeared, and perhaps elsewhere their bearing on my own can be assessed.

These pages are dedicated to the memory of two teachers who in differing but complementary ways saw deeply into the literary imagination: Arthur Darby Nock and Renato Poggioli.

Berkeley, California
5 April 1968

INTRODUCTION

This monograph presents two related sets of data. The first concerns the critical literary theory, "levels of intent," developed by scholars of the poetry of Catullus. Although it is a useful theory, it cannot be applied to all of Catullus' poems, and leads to ignoring certain of his poems. The second objective of this paper is to study certain poems of Catullus which the levels of intent theory has tended to pass over. These poems are examined according to the methods suggested by a critique of the theory of levels of intent. These poems are shown to possess unique character. The critical techniques which can explain them must be developed for each poem; a generalized theory about the poetry of Catullus is insufficient for thorough comprehension and evaluation of individual poems.

Poem 50 (pp. 1-7) is readily understandable as a text which does not rely upon metaphor to make its statement. However, it gains greatly in implication when linked to other poems of Catullus. In contrast, the significance of poem 30 (pp. 7-12) depends upon experiencing other poems in the corpus, although its use of images is restrained. Poem 65 (pp. 13-27) constitutes continuous metaphor. It presents a consistent intellectual statement in its images and forms a unified text. Poem 68 (27-51) relies upon an Alexandrian framework, "ring-composition," and is a model of a psychological state. It presents a unique and personal experience as a work of art and uses myth, formal structure and metaphor to express this experience.

Apart from the critical approaches suggested for each of these four poems, detailed criticism of these texts is offered. Further, attention is directed toward the complexities of Catullan criticism, and the significance and value for the critic of Catullus' practice of poetry.

A formal table of contents is not presented because the discussion of the four poems is continuous. However, comment centers upon the four texts on the pages mentioned above. The order of these four texts is established by the increasing complexity of the material, and the corresponding elaboration of the critical approach necessary to understand them. The order suggests nothing about the chronology.

ENARRATIO CATULLIANA:
CARMINA L, XXX, LXV, LXVIII

The concept of "levels of intent" suggested by J. P. Elder and developed by K. Quinn [1] has proved useful in determining how far criticism should probe a given poem of Catullus in attempting to explicate it. Just as it is obvious that poem 68 deserves the lengthy treatment recently accorded it, [2] so too the distich 85 cannot easily sustain a discussion fuller than that devoted to it by O. Weinreich. [3] Catullus is one of the most complex poets in any language. For one of his lyrics to constitute a profound poetical experience it is not necessary that it use imagery extensively or organize itself around symbolic statements in the mode of myth. To be sure, such techniques in a Catullan poem insure a relatively greater degree of seriousness. However, sophistication in metaphor built on complicated structure (technical competence) or supposed profundity of emotion or self insight (ultimately the shibboleth of sincerity) are not the only means of identifying a poem as worthy of deep critical analysis. [4] A poem's structure may be obvious, its use of imagery negligible, and its message accessible to all after a little effort in imagination. This hypothetical poem of low level intent may however present difficult critical problems and indeed defy total explication. Further, many of its details may refuse to give up the secret of their occurrence at such a place, in such a form, in such a poem. The recent investigations of M. C. J. Putnam [5]

---

[1] J. P. Elder, "Notes on some conscious and subconscious Elements in Catullus' Poetry," *HSCP* 60 (1951) 101-136; see especially 110: "... His purposes varied with the nature of the poem he set out to write." K. Quinn, *The Catullan Revolution* (Melbourne, 1959) especially 32-43.

[2] C. Lieberg, *Puella Divina: die Gestalt der göttlichen Geliebten bei Catull im Zusammenhang der antiken Dichtung*, (Amsterdam, 1962) 152 ff.

[3] O. Weinreich, *Die Distichen des Catull* (Tübingen, 1926) 37 ff.

[4] Quinn's "intervening stage" (can we never abandon a bent to order Catullus chronologically?) concerns poems "far from negligible structurally" such as c. 97; Quinn (cited in note 1 above) 36; cf. Elder (cited in note 1 above) 103 f. on c. 46. More recently Quinn acknowledges that a Catullan poem may be "more seriously poetic than the poet had in mind to begin with": K. F. Quinn, "Docte Catulle," *Critical Essays on Roman Literature: Elegy and Lyric*, ed. J. P. Sullivan (London, 1962) 33.

[5] M. C. J. Putnam, "The Art of Catullus 64," *HSCP* 65 (1961) 156-205; "Catullus' Journey: carm. 4," *CP* 57 (1962) 10-19.

acknowledge this problem by selecting for discussion a poem whose questions can best be resolved by reference to other poems thought to be related through poetical technique and topic to the central one under study.

Yet there are poems of Catullus, more or less like the hypothetical poem just mentioned, whose real problems must be solved by other means than either determining their level of intent or elucidating their relationships with other poems. Four such texts occupy this discussion: *50, 30, 65,* and *68.*[1] Each of these embodies in varying degrees critical problems of formal analysis as well as of the nature of Catullus' poetry. Formally these are an exoteric occasional poem (50), another so private as to make discursive treatment difficult (30), an introductory poem to a translation from Callimachus (65), and an elegiac "epyllion," (68). Considered from the standpoint of poetical sophistication they are increasingly complex and symbolic, though the "level of intent" in the first two is relatively low. If the critic confined himself to a depth of analysis suggested by the level of intent in these texts, he would not so quickly confront their problematical structure and significance.

In each of these poems the *I*, whom it is reasonable to call Catullus, is in conflict; conflict is the tenor of the poems (particularly *50* and *30*) but remains ambiguous in terms of the individual texts. Appeals for other poems to provide grounds of inference about the poet's unhappiness are not lacking. Thus Alfenus of c. 30 is conjecturally linked to P. Alfenus Varus who *may* be the Varus of *10* and *22.*[2] The situation of disappointed friendship adumbrated in *30* is not unlike that in *38, 73,* and *77.*[3] As for c. 50, Catullus' relations with C. Licinius Calvus (that gifted orator of a great family) can be amplified by referring to *14* and *53.* But all the external data about Calvus that one could wish for will not reveal why Catullus makes use of an erotic vocabulary to characterize his feelings of loss, nor will reference to other poems where Catullus'

---

[1] G. Jachmann, "Dieses Schibboleth des Catull-interpreten," *Gnomon* I (1925) 209. The four poems are presented in this order to facilitate critical discussion. Nothing is implied about their chronology.

[2] C. J. Fordyce, *Catullus: a Commentary* (Oxford, 1961) *ad. loc.* For further views on Alfenus' identity see R. Ellis, *A Commentary on Catullus*[2] (Oxford 1889) *ad loc.*; M. Lenchantin de Gubernatis, *Il Libro di Catullo Veronese* (Turin, 1928) *ad loc.* is honest: attempted identifications "non sono che congetture." See also page 8, note 2 below.

[3] *C. Valerius Catullus* ed. W. Kroll[4] (Stuttgart, 1960) *ad loc.*

pietas plays a role[1] throw light on the complex movement of thought in *30*. The fact that other poems of Catullus have pictures of comparison at their conclusions[2] does not explain why c. 65 seems badly integrated, or, if developed along the lines of a subtle inner harmony with c. 66, why it uses the image it does at the end. The difficulties of *68* are well-known. These and other concomitant problems are real enough to claim attention.

Poem 50, a superficially lucid and perennially delightful lyric, is freer of images than *30* or *65*. This poem's intellectual statement is that Catullus is not where he wants to be, namely with Calvus, and is therefore unhappy. The construction is equally direct. The first six lines lift the poem from the rank of personal communication to the status of true *Gelegenheitsgedicht*.[3] Catullus evidently intended this to be a public poem, and to find a place in his corpus. Lines 7 through 17 reveal the poet's sadness. The concluding section, beginning with *nunc* (as do many of Catullus' conclusions) [4] introduces Nemesis, a higher power whom it would be better not to offend. Calvus' recollection of Nemesis, furthered by this poem, will keep Catullus' requests from being neglected. The tripartite division corresponds to narration of a real situation (explaining the context of the whole poem), a subjective account of interior private feeling, and a prayer (an attempt to achieve through language something not yet made explicit in the material world nor yet within oneself). It is not clear what *preces nostras* (line 18) are; if taken to mean the concluding lines of the poem, '[quod] oramus,' which technically are not prayer but valediction, only a little sense is gained. Further, *hoc poema* cannot be the prayer of the poet for it makes no request. Only his desire to see the dawn is expressed, 'ut tecum loquerer simulque ut essem' (13). How can Calvus know in respect to what he must beware of slighting Nemesis? The poem's opening has turned the poem from Calvus' own to the common property of all who read it. Calvus has no

---

[1] E.g., *76*, the end of *50*, Ariadne's lament in *64*.

[2] See U. von Wilamowitz-Moellendorff, *Reden u. Vorträge*[3] (Berlin, 1913) 268-69 and note; cf. Catullus *2, 11, 17, 25*; Vergil *Georg.* 1; Horace *Ars p.*; Theocritus *7, 12*.

[3] E. Fraenkel, *Horace* (Oxford, 1957) 314. Quinn, "Docte Catulle" 60 n. 1, (page 1, note 4 above) lists c. 50 as typical of Catullus' best.

[4] See e.g., c. 3.11; 4.25; 8.16; 17.23; 21.10; 30.9; 39.17; 45.19; etc. The force of *nunc* varies from poem to poem, as one might expect; see page 11, note 2 below.

inside information, only the text which the reader also possesses.

It has been presumed that Catullus' petition (*preces* is a bit elevated in tone) is for another meeting with Calvus.[1] It is comfortable to take the most obvious interpretation; but to do so here means that the adversative *at* of line 14, and what follows it through the end of Catullus' self-representation, is to be downgraded in importance. Clearly *hoc poema* replaces Catullus' intense desire[2] 'ut tecum loquerer simulque ut essem.' Or better, the poem fulfills Catullus' wish: it speaks to Calvus and is close to him as its author perforce is not. After the manic thrashing on the bed[3] the tired limbs find repose as the mind clears, the obfuscations growing from frustration are dissipated, and Catullus writes *hoc poema*, 'ex quo perspiceres meum dolorem.' Poetry as a result of labor was as well known to the neoterics as to Horace, but c. 50 is only indirectly the result of *labor*, suffering. It is more a fictive spontaneous statement (offered to Calvus) arising after the effects of *labor*, which set in because of Calvus, have passed off. To be sure, *preces nostras* refers on one level of meaning to being again with Calvus who was universally known as Catullus' greatest friend.[4] But more far-reaching meanings can be elicited.

A poem may have meanings in addition to those conferred upon it by its author. Recent soundings for the meaning in Catullus of the *domus*,[5] of travel,[6] of the dead brother,[7] and of the poet's preoccupation with himself as female[8] are useful. Drawing connections between various poems along psychological or symbolic lines

---

[1] See Fordyce for an uncritical acceptance of this view; Kroll is more reserved: *"Preces*, deren Inhalt nicht ganz klar ist . . . C. kann wohl nur meinen, dass Calvus heute wieder mit ihm zusammenkommen soll." Cf. Ellis: "The poem may be practically considered a return-invitation." Lenchantin is as reserved as Kroll: "Quali esse sieno non dice il poeta, . . . ma si inferisce che procede . . ."

[2] Lenchantin is precise in his explicitness: Catullus is "in uno stato d'orgasmo." For the sensual implications, as perhaps in c. 31.9, see Putnam, *CP* 57 (1962) 18 n. 8. He also stresses Catullus' intimacy with Calvus: 'ocelle,' *op. cit.* 12.

[3] Perhaps Yeats had this in mind when he wrote "The Scholars."

[4] Lenchantin *ad. loc.*

[5] Putnam, *HSCP* 65 (1961) 183, 191, 196; *CP* 57 (1962) 57 n. 13. Elder (cited in note 1 page 1 above) 129 f.

[6] Putnam, *HSCP* 65 (1961) 168.

[7] Putnam, *HSCP* 65 (1961) 183, 186.

[8] Elder (cited page 1, note 1 above) 131; Putnam, *HSCP* 65 (1961) 170, 198, 202 n. 28.

creates an auxiliary structure: an indispensable one, perhaps even a beautiful construction, but distinctly secondary as compared to the independent freestanding texts themselves. The individual poems are literary occurrences in a special way; their mutual heightenings and shadowings are less so. Profoundest meaning may be elicited from the whole, or may be infused from without. An originally viable sturdy text is necessary. Otherwise the poem, overfreighted with semantical and philosophical lumber, will be lost to sight.

Just as the opening of c. 50 provides certain essential facts for the reader to comprehend, so too does the core of this text, lines 7-17. These eleven lines (counting the literally transitional 7) are further divided by *at*, line 14. The placing of this line is deliberate: of the 21 lines in the poem it is the fourteenth; of the eleven lines of the core, it occurs after seven lines, before the final three; $(13 + 7) = 2 (7 + 3)$. The seven lines before *at* show the poet suffering the traditional symptoms of lovesickness such as "me miserum,' displeasure with food, inability to sleep, heightened nervous restlessness, and frustration. After the fit has passed, the poet's exhausted limbs find repose, and he writes this address which pictures his *dolor* to his friend in erotic terms. The two personal verbs of the opening, *lusimus* and *ludebat*, are also erotic. *ludere* means to write love poetry as well as to make love.[1] Calvus and Catullus in their sporting and drinking have engaged in a spontaneous competition of love poetry 'ut convenerat esse delicatos.' [2] Catullus, inflamed, longs to repeat his afternoon. Calvus must have invited his friend for the afternoon: both are explicitly *otiosi*, and evenings for the ancients were regularly free. Further, Catullus attempts to eat upon returning home, an action hardly consonant with an evening party at a great house. It is natural that Catullus phrases his intense picture of his frenzied suffering in the language of the epigrams and other amorous *paignia* that he has recently been bandying with Calvus. The person addressed by the suffering poet is traditionally the one who causes distress, frequently by denying access. Hence the mock-solemn plea for steadfastness at the end.

---

[1] *Pace* Fordyce on *68*. 17; see Jachmann, *Gnomon* I (1925) 211, and page 35, note 1 below.

[2] "Naughty" (Fordyce) is absurd; *delicatus* means *lascivus*, or even *mollis*: wanton, reckless, heedless, impulsively feminine or femininely impulsive in erotic situations.

So read, poem 50 forms an intelligible unit. But another level of meaning is present in the poem. Just as for most Roman poets it is impossible to write without striking an attitude,[1] so for Catullus, ridden as he was by "Lesbia," and in a certain sense made the poet he was by her, love expressions and powerful recurrent symbols are never for long lacking.[2] Can one confidently assert that Lesbia did not figure in the *tabellae* written at Calvus' house? It would be strange if she did not. Words which recall her, or what she represented, were present to some extent whenever the poet turned toward love poetry. When Catullus leaves Calvus' house, his troubles set in. He has exchanged a happy *domus* for one where he sleeps alone ('toto lecto versarer'). Just as in the even more complex c. 68, Catullus' brother and his beloved move clearly into focus and then shift into Laodamia and Troy,[3] so in the less closely textured c. 50 the shadow of the absent lover falls across *preces nostras*: "keep faith with me."[4] Lesbia no doubt must often have been more directly responsible for such sleeplessness as that set forth in c. 50. (Catullus' address to himself to set his house in order, c. 8, shows how he can represent his resolve to face facts as a resolve fluctuating in the space of a few lines. It ebbs away as the questions grow more particularly intimate, and is manfully summoned back stronger than before at line 19.) In returning to his own house in c. 50, Catullus enters a *domus* which is less than perfect. Hence he intensely desires to return to the *domus* where he was happy, where he encountered a lover 'meis tabellis.' One recalls how large the *domus* of Manlius (or Allius) looms in c. 68, 155 f.: 'sitis felices et tu simul et tua vita,/et domus [ipsa] in qua lusimus et domina.'

C. Licinius Calvus in c. 50 is addressed not only as a friend of the poet, but also as the poet's beloved. The strong language of *50*, 'tuo lepore incensus,' lines 7-8, is comparable to 'mei lepores' in the occasional poem to Ipsitilla, c. 32. Catullus writes to Calvus out of some love relationship. Calvus may be the poet's surrogate for Lesbia in a humorous exaggeration. Or he may share a homosexual passion. What is important is that Catullus introduces into this poem many strong elements which poems directly concerning

---

[1] E. A. Havelock, *The Lyric Genius of Catullus* (Oxford, 1939) 95.

[2] See notes 5-8, page 4 above and the end of note 1, page 12 below.

[3] See especially Elder (cited in page 1, note 1 above) 129 ff; and 30 ff. below.

[4] See c. 76, which is a prayer.

Lesbia also exhibit. Poem 50 is a free-spirited, playfully extravagant account of how Catullus missed Calvus' amusing company, together with a plea for him to forswear boldness and remain faithful in the relationship which he and Catullus have created, whatever it may have been. It is simultaneously the poet's coming to terms with the frustration of love existing only through words not deeds, and a cry for constancy on the part of his lover and of himself too. When he was not *delicatus*, 'defessa labore membra. . . semimortua lectulo iacebant.' His love is the source for his life's movements: 'toto . . . lecto versarer.' Hence he exclaims to himself, to Calvus and to his readers, 'precesque nostras,/ oramus, cave despuas, ocelle.' Keeping faith was for Catullus as important as keeping alive, and perhaps both the reason for continuing existence and the means for doing so. Poem 50 does not use the symbolic mode but itself constitutes a symbol, its text being a metaphor, the deepest significance of which as always for Catullus blends into a key symbol of his life: here, the *foedus amicitiae*.

Poem 50 precedes one of the greatest efforts of Catullus, the Sapphic ode 'Ille mi par esse deo videtur.' In a similar way another ambiguous poem, c. 30, precedes the majestic 'Paene insularum.' Though Catullus is probably not responsible for this ordering, both *50* and *30*, poems of deceptive clarity and intense personal preoccupation, are followed by the poet's more public utterance, which is profound. Yet deep-lying meanings can be elicited without undue strain.[1] The broad movement of thought in *30* is parallel to that of *50*. The poet, in conflict and sadness, addresses a friend (or former friend), begs not to be forgotten (or complains about forgetfulness) and refers to divine remembrance in an attempt to caution against recklessly dismissing his petition. While c. 50 uses no metaphorical images but rather is itself metaphor, c. 30 uses them in a restrained form. They carry the sense but are themselves camouflaged. Hence arise the difficulties which the commentators have encountered in *30*.[2] To write a dozen lines in a meter as

---

[1] On c. 51 see W. Ferrari, "Il carme 51 di Catullo," *Annali della R. Scuola Normale Superiore di Pisa (Lettere, Storia e Filosofia)* Ser. II, 7 (1938) 59-72; for c. 31, Putnam, *CP* 57 (1962) 10 ff.

[2] E.g., ". . . terms so general . . . as to give no clue to their occasion" (Fordyce); "nur an Alfenus richtet" (Kroll); Ellis is most conservative: he avoids the question of this poem's accessibility to the reader, though he recognizes that the language of the poem needs explanation.

difficult as the greater Asclepiadean for the eyes of a false friend is inefficient. In its way *30* is as exoteric as *31*.[1] It is not necessary to know who Alfenus is in order to perceive the conflict which the poet represents himself undergoing. Indeed, Catullus makes artistic use of keeping back from his audience the exact nature of his betrayal. To be undone by so shadowy an adversary is more effective than to relate circumstantial details. Alfenus, by his very lack of definite and perhaps banal identity, grows into a question-mark: "who among staunch friends was the weak one?" Also, by omitting the specific reasons for his unhappiness, the poet leaves it all the more problematical and unbounded, and hence can develop aspects of self-pity without running the risk of appearing to exaggerate. Further factual information about Alfenus, welcome though it would be, could not alter the tension caused by the text's order of words. *A fortiori*, it could emerge that Alfenus had provoked c. 30 by forgetting Catullus' birthday, or that he was the P. Alfenus Varus, *consul suffectus*, in 39, of Horace *Sat.* I. 3. 130[2] and that his desire to change his station in life had disappointed his compatriot. Such new evidence would indeed form a new context and would compel a new reading of the poem. But it would not invalidate a criticism which still took *30* as a serious complaint. For that was what the poet wrote. An addressee is required by poems of smaller dimensions and intentions. Catullus departs from the tradition only in c. 10, which is addressed to no one and to nothing, not even the poet. Alfenus may be named only to fulfill a generic obligation.[3]

---

[1] Elder (cited page 1, note 1 above) 129 compares c. 30 with *76*; he is surely right in saying that Alfenus is nothing more sensational than Catullus' friend. It is interesting to note that Lipsius thought c. 30 was an allegory, with Cicero as Catullus, Pompey as Alfenus; see Ellis *ad loc.*

[2] Klebs, *RE* I 2 (1394) 1472-73: "Nach Zeit u. Heimat kann er der Alfenus sein an der Catull c. 30 richtet." Broughton *MRR* II lists P. Alfenus P. f. Varus as *consul suffectus* for 39 and cites Dig. 1. 2. 2. 44 and Porph. on Horace *Sat.* 1. 3. 130; Broughton further lists P. Alfenus Varus as a legate, lieutenant (or perhaps iiivir) of Caesar's distributing land to veterans in Cisalpine Gaul in 41 (see under Legates, Lieutenants [376] and Special Commission [377-78]). He was of senatorial rank, perhaps *praetor* in 42 (see 529). Apparently his local origin is unknown. He is the Varus of Vergil *Buc.* 6. 10-12; 26-27, known to the poet through his work as *iiivir agris dividendis*.

[3] Cf. Weinrich (cited above page 1, note 3) 44; he mentions as well fear of being alone. It is remotely possible that Catullus has so completely assumed the *persona* of Ariadne that a male addressee is needed; see page 10, note 36 below.

The chief device of poem 30 is an alternation between human sorrow and divine awareness of it. The first four lines state this theme briefly; lines 5-6 phrase the problem in a seemingly general way, and introduce 7-12, which examine permutations of it from the specific point of view of the betrayed lover. The only proper names in this poem are the shadowy Alfenus and Fides, a "spirit of good faith." [1] Fides is as unspecific a figure as Alfenus but one whose function is more readily accessible to the reader than is the addressee's. Alfenus may well be taken as standing for an anti-Fides. Kroll stresses Alfenus' passiveness in another way: "Alfenus, der C.'s Vertrauen getäuscht hat, nicht so sehr durch eine Schlechtigkeit als durch eine Unterlassung." If a sin of omission is more central to *30*, what are the *facta* which are mentioned three times (lines 4, 9, 12), more than any other noun? His action may have been clearer to Catullus and Catullus' immediate public. Whatever it was, it gives the poet scope to characterize his conflicts.

Briefly, three themes common to other poems of Catullus succeed each other rapidly: the themes of *pietas*, of Ariadne and of the broken promise. Reference to other poems of Catullus is essential in this case, not to understand the direction and tenor of the poet's language, but to grasp all its implications. The first four lines show the poet's *pietas*: he has been *dulcis amiculus*, a constant friend, not seeking the limits of his freedom. He is betrayed callously, and such wicked deeds do not please heaven. This idea is represented in a more leisurely way and examined in a more complex poem, c. 76. In it Catullus, again the injured party in this dialectic of intense friendship sanctioned by the gods[2] (surely with Lesbia in *76*), characterizes his *pietas* in the same terms as he uses to reveal Alfenus' failure: 'foedere nullo/divum ad fallendos numine abusum homines' (76. 3-4); 'me prodere, . . . non dubites fallere' (30. 3); 'quaecumque homines bene cuiquam aut dicere possunt/aut facere' (76. 7-8); 'dicta omnia factaque' (30. 9). As Lesbia was lacking in *76*, so Alfenus in *30* has not kept his promise to Catullus and could be accused 'violasse fidem.' The nature of the gods'

---

[1] So Fordyce; Lenchantin says, " . . . può essere la Buona Fede divinità venerata sul Campidoglio" or perhaps "la fede giurata, la sacra promessa di amicizia calpestata da Alfeno."

[2] On the *foedus amicitiae* see the admirable article by R. Reitzenstein, "Zur Sprache der lateinischen Erotik," *Sitzungsberichte der Heidelberger Akademie, Phil.-Hist. Kl.*, 1912, pp. 3-36.

protection of such contracts is best seen in 76, but the double thread of human sorrow and divine recognition runs through 30 as well. The seemingly general statement in lines 5-6 is in reality fully specific; the key words are *neglegis, deseris in malis*, and the poignant questions of line 6.

Carmen 64. 132-301, Ariadne's lament,[1] offers many parallels: *perfide* (132, 133) and *30. 3*; *deserto* (133) and *deseris* (*30. 5*); *neglecto numine divum* (134) and *neglegis* (*30. 5*), *caelicolis* (*30. 4*); *iubebas* (140) and *30. 7*; *cuncta irrita venti* (142) and *omnia ventos irrita* (*30. 9-10*); *fallaci* (150) and *fallacum* (*30. 4*); *externata malo* (165) and *miserum in malis* (*30. 5*); *quo me referam?* (177) and *eheu quid faciant?* (*30. 6*); *facta virum multantes Eumenides* (192-193) and *facta impia fallacum* [*non*] *caelicolis placent* (*30. 4*), *di meminerunt, meminit Fides* (*30. 11*).[2] Lines 3-12 of c. 30 could be spoken by Ariadne without change (except of course of gender, 'miseram' line 5). But principally lines 5-8 can with justice be said to be significantly related to the Ariadne complex.[3] The parallels in the "epyllion" for 'neglegis, deseris in malis, iubebas tradere animam, nunc dicta omnia factaque ventos irrita ferre sinis' would alone be sufficient to demonstrate this relationship, even without the parallel sequences which ask in whom faith may now be safely reposed. The import is clear enough. Catullus' misery is love misery. He has been abandoned cruelly, and from his standpoint unnecessarily rejected. There is no cogent reason for supposing that this abandonment was not the betrayal of his life, Lesbia's desertion. While c. 30 shares key themes and expressions with the section of c. 64 which represents Ariadne's lament it also participates in what may be called the broken promise syndrome.[4] One of Catullus'

---

[1] Ariadne's lament is carefully discussed by Putnam, *HSCP* 65 (1961) 167 ff.

[2] If one includes the passage introducing Ariadne's lament, specifically lines 55-75, the following parallels appear: *fallaci* (*somno*) (55), *fallacum* (*hominum*) (*30. 4*); *desertam* (57), *deseris* (*30. 5*); *se miseram* (57), *me miserum* (*30. 5*); *immemor* (58), *immemor* (*30. 1*); *irrita ventosae linquens promissa procellae* (59), *ventos irrita ac nebulas aereas sinis* (*30. 10*). I omit not a few from lines 76-131 and 202-264, the section concluding Ariadne's lament. These words and phrases are part of the rhetoric of complaint, but their appearance in precisely these two poems is neither fortuitous nor a result of Catullus' supposed narrow range of expression.

[3] For Catullus as Ariadne see Putnam, *HSCP* 65 (1961) 170, 198, and page 4, note 8 above.

[4] On the intellectual background, see Reitzenstein, cited page 9, note 2 above; one is tempted to take c. 87 literally. Compare c. 109. 5 f. Putnam,

favorite devices is contrasting then and now; *nunc*[1] frequently introduces the unpleasant reality of present time.[2] The more remote time is generally the more desirable and the present is the time of unfulfillment, of the broken vow. Such is the case in c. 30. Before *nunc* the poet gave himself wholeheartedly to love, without a thought for danger. Alfenus withdraws himself or withholds himself ('nunc retrahis te') and the act *tradere animam* is undone, together with Alfenus' *facta* and *dicta*. What the *dicta* were can be inferred from the text: "I bid you love without fear, surrender your soul to her, all is safe; it is I who tell you this." The stressing of Alfenus, 'tute iubebas,' implies that Alfenus was reasonably thought more than competent to give such advice to Catullus, out of some special knowledge of the situation in which the poet found himself. He is surprised at betrayal from that quarter. When Alfenus' benevolent action ceases, Catullus' position is intolerable. It is natural to infer that the affection to which Catullus makes reference in c. 30 is not for Alfenus but for another. Alfenus in some way was necessary for a rapprochement with the beloved. Perhaps his role was not unlike that of Allius as set down in c. 68, in which case Alfenus was either not innocent of trickery or a fool. *Carmen* 30 implies the former. Alfenus' guilty action was *iubere animam tradere*, and his *dicta* perhaps not unlike those which Ariadne attributes to the cruel Theseus: 'sperare iubebas conubia laeta, optatos hymenaeos.' If it is imagined that Alfenus out of malice and treachery, and perhaps not without the woman's connivance, bade the poet to hope for a permanent liason, c. 30 becomes clear in meaning. Alfenus is responsible to the gods not so much because he is a principal party to this *foedus amicitiae* but because he is its disingenuous instigator. By disassociating himself from this lovers' compact he caused it to break.[3]

HSCP 65 (1961) 170 called c. 30 a "stray example" of an episode in Catullus' life which may have caused him to assume the *persona* of Ariadne; apparently he did not consider the possibility of Lesbia's lying behind c. 30.

[1] *Nunc* or some such word, as by implication *ut ante* in c. 11. 21 and the concluding section of *64* (397 ff.).

[2] Some examples are: c. *3*. 11; *8*. 9 and 16; *21*. 10; *58*. 4; *72*. 5; *78b*. 1; *101*. 7; see page 3, note 4 above and compare Putnam, *HSCP* 65 (1961) 175. On the time mechanics of c. 68, see pages 43 f. below.

[3] Lesbia thus may have had in Alfenus (as she did with her husband Metellus Celer until 59) a way out of her affair with Catullus. Catullus may have been exacerbated only by Alfenus' offering and then withdrawing

Perhaps Catullus in c. 30 is not yet ready to face the fact that he faces in c. 76, that his love for Lesbia was *taeter morbus*; perhaps he was just on the verge of the mental outlook set down in c. 8, but could as yet blame neither himself nor Lesbia for his passion's undoing.[1] It is also possible that Catullus could not write of any friendship's ending without picking up the threads leading to his passion for Lesbia. According to this view, c. 30 would be simply an overly strong statement of Catullus' feeling for Alfenus' treachery, a poem which only by misdirection, misapplication of the Ariadne echoes, leads the reader to Lesbia. If Catullus cannot mention Troy without his brother's death coming to the surface of his thoughts (as in c. 68) perhaps the same thing is true of fidelity, which automatically produces the complex of Lesbia and treachery. But poems are not reflex actions; even a consummate artist must by trial and error arrive at his fair copy. Enough control is insured by the time necessary to write a poem in a complex quantitative metrical pattern such as the greater Asclepiadean to obviate chance intrusion. If Lesbia's aura in c. 30 was originally intrusion, its presence there now is no oversight on Catullus' part. It seems more probable that Alfenus, whoever he was, functions in c. 30 as a surrogate for the beloved, or Lesbia. The poet does not attack her as in c. 11; he attacks her through her pawn, and in so doing reveals his own wretchedness. Such a hypothesis clarifies this ambiguous text.[2]

---

help, such as use of his house for the liason. But this leaves *iubere animam tradere* largely unexplained.

[1] Ellis on c. 30 alludes to the possibility of connecting Alfenus with the Lesbia affair, but believes that the view that "Alfenus is himself the object of the friendship here described, is, on the whole, more consistent with the general scope of the poem;" however, he cites *64*. 141, "the passionate complaint of Ariadne," as parallel for *30*. 9-10. Kroll offers this: "dass [c. 30] mit dem Verhältnis zu Lesbia etwas zu tun hat, ist möglich, aber durch nichts angedeutet." Merrill, *Catullus* (1893; reprinted Cambridge, Mass., 1951) invites comparison with c. 38, and thinks that connecting it to the Lesbia episode would be "a forced interpretation of vv. 7-8." Lenchantin offers a conjecture that perhaps Alfenus had been conquered with love for Lesbia: which in view of Catullus' restrained language in *30* is unlikely, as Ellis thought. It is possible that Catullus had feelings for another as strong as those for Lesbia. But it is not intruding either Lesbia or biographical criticism to use her name for the greatly beloved woman.

[2] The tense word order of line 11 (Kroll calls it "verzwickt") is undoubtedly due to this difficult meter with its demand for a double diaeresis. But perhaps it owes as much to the poet's setting down a tentative state of mind; note too the way 'meminerunt, meminit' is re-inforced by 'facti

If c. 50 functions as a real occasional poem without recourse to images, and if c. 30 uses restrained and camouflaged images and touchstones, held in common with other Catullan poems, to carry the reader toward the sense, c. 65 is entirely founded on metaphor. In it image, total metaphor, is supreme. It is curious that c. 65 has provoked so little examination. The only continuous discussion of it was written well over half a century ago by Wilamowitz.[1] He perceived the complexity of the language and structure and felt that Catullus desired to parallel in his introduction to c. 66 the complexities of thought in the *Lock* itself. According to Wilamowitz, the poet's grief is real, but not stronger than his will to express himself. The surprising address to his brother does not fit into the letter form very well, and brings about a second address to Ortalus. The commonplace conclusion with its lively tone (in motif an echo of Callimachus' Cydippe) ill accords with the whole, Wilamowitz asserted. His thoughtful remark on the conclusion of c. 65 is worth quotation: "Die eingenügende Verzahnung der selbstandig ausgearbeiteten Teile ist bei Catull oft zu bemerken, und an den Schluss eines Gedichtes ein Gleichnis oder sonst ein Bild zu setzen, ist ein gern geübten Kunstgriff."[2] But this does not suggest why the particular picture was chosen, or why the images of poetry, death and forgetting are *fetus, unda* and *malum*. There is more than an intellectual unity imposed by the reader. In connection with this point it is useful to recall what Wilamowitz said concerning the nature of Catullan poetry: it was written for reading aloud, especially by the poet himself.[3] Hence the striving for changes in tone stands the reciter in good stead but shocks the "verständigen Leser." *Verstandsbildung* confers the power to follow ideas but makes it awkward for the leaps of voice and sense. It is difficult to grasp a literary production which demands such complicated preconditions; it is beyond one's powers of adaptability to adjust successfully to such an incongruous statement.[4] This is eminently true up to a point, as all who read Catullus and try

---

faciet': the shadowy crime of Alfenus is surely more than one of forgetting. See page 11, note 3 above.

[1] U. von Wilamowitz-Moellendorff (cited page 3, note 2 above) 267-270, the conclusion of his article on c. 66 (which ultimately goes back as far as 1879).

[2] Wilamowitz, 268.

[3] Wilamowitz, 269. This is most important for c. 68, as will be shown.

[4] Wilamowitz, 269.

to explicate him can see. But more can be said to suggest why
certain leaps occur when they do and how the reader who abdicates
his discursive outlook may penetrate the metaphors which are
the ultimate sense as well as the form of such a poem as c. 65.[1]

Poem 65 is syntactically a prodosis introduced by *etsi*, and an
apodosis beginning with *sed tamen*, line 15. Each segment of this
arch contains an apparent digression: in the prodosis the *nam*
clause containing reference to the brother's death; in the apodosis
the *ut* clause with its comparison of the young girl forgetful of
her lover's gift. Digression is not the right word, however. The
death of the brother, though syntactically subordinate, is most
important in sense, for it is why the poet is not at Rome, and
accounts for his inability to comply with Ortalus' request.[2] It
occupies ten lines out of twenty-four (including the missing hexa-
meter, line 9). Its pendant, the *ut* clause of 19 ff., takes up six
lines. Of the remaining eight lines, four are the *etsi* clause proper,
four the *sed tamen* clause. By sheer weight the *nam* and *ut* con-
structions are of consequence; also the *nam* clause is intellectually
central, as just seen. The *ut* comparison is no less vital, and is
hardly a "charmingly vivid and unexpected simile" (Fordyce)
but rather is metaphoric, symbolic thought of the highest order.
All four segments of this poem combine to give it its symbolic
form: death and rebirth.

To consider these interlocking segments in the order in which
they unfold in the audience's consciousness is important. It must
be borne in mind that the sum of any poem, not least this one,
is greater than its parts. In this instance, key words grow in impact
only after the end of the poem is achieved. The first two lines,
if read aloud, could be a conventional lover's complaint:[3] *cura*
frequently in Catullus means the trials and sorrows of love.[4]

---

[1] Quinn says next to nothing about c. 65, and Fordyce offers little.
Of the other commentators, Kroll understandably follows Wilamowitz
("den Stil des folgenden Gedichtes nachzuahmen"); Ellis says little useful
here. Lenchantin is not without interest: c. 65 "è costituita da un solo
periodo che procede non senza stento . . . ma l'andamento sintattico lento e
impacciato ritrae gli intimi moti del cuor del poeta che, prostrato dalla
sventura, pare, che a fatica riesca a fissare il suo pensiero."

[2] Cf. Putnam, *HSCP* 65 (1961) 178.

[3] See the opening of the Ciris: 'etsi me vario iactatum laudis amore/ irrita-
que expertum fallacis praemia vulgi . . .'

[4] *Carmen* 2. 10 (see Kroll); *64.* 62; *64.* 250; *68.* 18 (just before the brother's
death is mentioned [cf. *64.* 95]); *68.* 51; perhaps even *31.* 7. Mynors' reading

The second couplet amplifies the verb, *sevocat*, in a striking way. The thought of the poet's mind (the tone of *mens animi* is distinctly elevated) cannot break out the sweet fruits of the Muses; it itself ebbs and flows, 'fluctuat tantis malis.' It is instructive to compare several passages in c. 68: 'cuius ego interitu tota de mente fugavi/ haec studia atque omnes delicias animi.' Here *haec studia*, erotic verse, are but one aspect of the poet's activity impeded by his brother's death. As subsequent discussion will show, c. 68. 11 ff. is an open discursive statement addressed to a person who had asked Catullus for some neoteric poetry ('munera et Musarum et Veneris.' 68.10). Catullus explains his incapacity in terms of his grief for his brother's death. The objective situations of *65* and *68* are most similar; but Catullus chose to be completely metaphorical throughout *65*.[1]

If a poem is read aloud slowly enough, time is at the hearer's disposal for him to make a brief meditation as it were upon the sense and its sensory and intellectual implications. If a slight expansion of the opening of c. 65 is made along these lines, it develops that the death of the poet's brother is made specific only in lines 5-6; line 5 makes a strong adumbration, juxtaposing *gurgite* and *fratris*, but one must wait for the end of line 6, *pedem*, to be certain that one has the sense accurately. Thus the first four lines move from the possibility of this being a love-poem in ever-narrowing ranges of probability inexorably to the certainty of the death of the poet's brother. If one wanted to make a scheme of the successive reverberations in the hearer's mind as he listens to lines 1-5 for the first time it would look something like this (with *etsi* showing that more will follow and coloring these words with the expectancy of the adversative):

line 1: love-pain (or perhaps other pain)
line 2: keeps him from cultivating the sources of (neoteric) poetry;
line 3: it cannot bring forth a new growth from stock put by (in better times),
line 4: —his mind, that is, cannot; it itself ebbs and flows ceaselessly out of some great disturbance.

---

confectum is generally accepted; for the Vatican Ottobonianus *defectum*, see Merrill *ad loc*.

[1] *Fluctuat* looks to *68*. 13: 'accipe, quis merser fortunae fluctibus ipse' (the death of his brother). *68* is, however, a more complex poem than *65*, as will emerge; its introduction, however, is more open.

Then in lines 5-6, in a tumble of words exploding in the audience's consciousness, the impediment is revealed. If the impact of the word order is observed, it will be seen that *me* is as far from *virginibus* as possible in this syntactical arrangement; as far as Catullus is from his Muses. *fetus*, young growing things recently come to light, is juxtaposed to *mens animi* by enjambement. *fetus expromere* is the most intimate and proper function of this poet's mind. Ortalus had addressed him in that role.[1] The lines which particularize *tantis malis* are most carefully wrought. In line 5 *mei* must leap over *nuper Lethaeo gurgite* in order to embrace *fratris*, must pass over what separates Catullus from his brother: a little space of time, the great expanse of death. The word order of lines 5-6 is disjointed and complex, shadowing forth Catullus' state of mind, and creating it anew momentarily in the audience. Finally it settles into an irrevocable factual statement when *pedem*, crucial for the syntax, sounds forth.

Characteristically for Catullus, only one aspect of the brother is touched upon, namely, his foot. The foot for Catullus is especially associated with the journey, and for Catullus' reader it is closely tied to c. 46. 8: 'iam laeti studio pedes vigescunt' and the inverted arrangement of the epiphany of the *puella divina*, 68. 70 ff.: 'quo mea se molli candida diva pede/ intulit.' [2] The foot upon which his brother began his journey to Troy (note the juxtaposition of *pedem* to *Troia*, lines 6-7) was not lucky and now the trickling wave of death breaks gently over its pallor. At this point there is established a correlative to 'mens animi fluctuat malis:' it is 'unda manans alluit pedem fratris mei.' A metaphoric identification of the two statements becomes desirable. The brother's death causes the poet's mind to be stirred ceaselessly. And while it *fluctuat* it is preoccupied with the death of the brother, and so absorbed it becomes what it thinks, and bodies itself forth in the image with which it pictures its preoccupation: *unda fluctuat*. Hence the apostrophe is not to a cenotaph in Italy or a Trojan tomb or to a remembrance of his brother but to the brother him-

---

[1] Cf. c. 68. 23-23: 'omnia tecum perierunt gaudia nostra,/ quae tuus in vita dulcis alebat amor.' Here the poet's brother has an active role in Catullus' *omnia gaudia*—not a random remark but a carefully controlled expression for the *persona* to wear at this point. See page 17, note 1 below.

[2] "...Departure haunted Catullus, meaning to him on most occasions little short of desertion." Putnam, *HSCP* 65 (1961) 168.

self, never to be seen again, in whose non-life Catullus through this poem is a momentary participant: 'numquam ego te... aspiciam posthac?' The question has an affirmative answer. He will try to recapture his dead brother in this way again: 'semper canam' (line 12), for his brother is *vita amabilior*. Though his brother is and will remain invisible ('subter litore tellus/ ereptum nostris obterit ex oculis,' lines 7-8) he will always love him. The *at* is a strong adversative, and borrows strength from the audience's expectation of an adversative to balance *etsi*; *at* however is not *the* adversative of the poem. One does not encounter it until line 15. One may wonder how well the overarching syntactical framework is kept in mind when hearing this poem for the first time; surely emphasis of voice would help. For instance, different tones could be used for each of the four sections, in order to show their interdependence as well as their individual wholeness.

'At certe semper amabo:' more than what Professor Nock has called "tendance of the dead" is what Catullus expresses here. Though the tomb is inaccessible and its occupant invisible, through art the poet has a means of communication with what he has lost. Similarly, every Lesbia poem that he wrote, even after the final rupture, was a way of touching Lesbia, of reaching her.

This almost Proustian theme is further developed in lines 13-14, the conclusion of both the *nam* explanatory excursus and of the *etsi* portion of the elegy. The songs which Catullus is to sing ('semper maesta tua carmina morte canam' is a corollary to 'semper amabo') will be 'qualia sub densis ramorum concinit umbris/ Daulias, absumpti fata gemens Ityli' (lines 13-14). Catullus never introduces pointless comparisons. This one is further particularization of his grief, and specifically the sorrow and profanation of Catullus' *domus* by death. A valuable adjunct is *68.* 21-22 (repeated in line 94): 'frater,/ tecum una tota est nostra sepulta domus.' Procne laments as nightingale her slain son.[1] Now Catullus as an ancient poet is

---

[1] *Daulias* in c. 65 can only be Procne. See J. Fontenrose, "The Sorrows of Ino and of Procne," *TAPA* 79 (1948), 125-167, especially 156-57, 130 f., and footnote 11, p. 131. Philomela is never wife of Tereus or mother of Ity(lu)s in either Greek or Roman poets. Procne is here the nightingale. Catullus doubtless plays upon dauliás/Dauliás in 'densis ramorum umbris.' See W. H. Roscher, *Ausführliches Lexicon der griechischen u. römischen Mythologie* s.v. Tereus (Leipzig, 1917). On *maeroribus*, Ellis cites Statius *Silv.* 5. 5. 8 (frantic grief for a dead adopted son) and *CIL* 1. 1202: 'interieisti et liquisti in maeroribus matrem.'

almost eccentric in his devotion to his brother. 'omnia tecum perierunt gaudia nostra' (*68*. 23), and 'iucundum lumen ademptum' (*68*. 93) are more like the epigraphical sentiments of a grieving parent than of a brother. *Carmen* 101, more of a public ritual poem, is correspondingly more restrained. Catullus' expression of love for Lesbia in *72*. 3-4 is also most unusual: 'dilexi tum te non tantum ut vulgus amicam/ sed pater ut gnatos diligit et generos,' (Propertius I. II. 23 notwithstanding.) Also pertinent is *64*. 215, Aigeus' words to Theseus just before the latter sails out of his father's life forever: 'gnate mihi longa iucundior unice vita.' [1]

The comparison of Catullus to Procne is not farfetched. For Catullus the most grievous act is the violation of the home. For instance, the fact that the brother's ashes lie 'non inter nota sepulcra/ nec prope cognatos' (*68*. 97-98) is a source of further grief.[2] Specifically lines 13-14 of c. 65 relate to the profanation of the home by death. The lament provoked thus will be song, the *carmina* of line 12 if not line 16. *Carmen* 66 is a poem of sundering and longing. Though obviously frivolous in spirit, it nevertheless could have suggested itself to Catullus at this particular juncture of his life because of its general topic. As Wilamowitz and Kroll have said, the structure of c. 65 is not unrelated to that of c. 66; one might say that in theme too they are comparable. If read out of context *66*. 21-22 is curious; even in context it is uncomfortably close to the delicate subject of the "covering letter:" 'et tu non orbum luxti deserta cubile,/ sed fratris cari flebile discidium?' Unfortunately comparison with Callimachus is impossible. At any rate Catullus' lament will be sung in deepest shadows of life, among growing things (*ramorum*) at their farthest remove from the sun of life.[3] The poet, experiencing the grief of brother, father and mother, will no longer be the same.

The *persona* of Catullus in his poems of higher intent is more

---

[1] Cf. Putnam, *HSCP* 65 (1961) 183 ff.

[2] E.g., the end of c. 64; see Putnam, *HSCP* 65 (1961) 196.

[3] Cf. c. 5. 6; *8*. 3, 8; esp. *68*. 16 'iucundum cum aetas florida ver egeret,/ multa satis lusi . . . sed totum hoc studium luctu fraterna mihi mors/ abstulit;' *lusi* refers to amatory verse such as Ortalus wanted; see Fraenkel, *Gnomon* 34 (1962) 262 and references there; Elder, page 1, n. 1 above, 130. The words quoted from *68* are from the poet's "letter" to Allius, a discursive statement of his life's *peripeteia*. But the metaphorical content of this line closely parallels c. 65. 3 ff. Catullus constantly juxtaposes love-poetry and his brother's death.

fluid than one might expect in a poet of such intense personal feeling and in the master of representing the emotions. In various poems and in differing ways Catullus metaphorically is identified with (that is to say poetically "is") his *phaselus*, Attis, Ariadne, and his own various poetic selves. Thus in c. 65 he is momentarily Procne.

In the *etsi* section of the poem Catullus abdicates the role of poet whose *mens animi* rejoices in *dulcis Musarum expromere fetus* and becomes the nightingale who sings lament because it is her nature to do so; she has no choice, and neither does Catullus. She has been transformed into the instrument of expressing her grief. She herself has become the metaphor of her grief. Her past not only causes her to become a nightingale but also gives her that which she must lament without ceasing, her dead son. "Even though" this has happened, even in *tantis maeroribus* (line 15; cf. *tantis . . . malis*, line 4) still Catullus as poet-bird keeps faith with Ortalus as with his brother. The words which Catullus uses to express his desire that Ortalus not regard his *dicta*, his claims upon Catullus' talents, as forgotten and invalid, are part of the "broken promise syndrome:" 'ne tua dicta vagis nequiquam credita ventis.' The following lines are analogous: in c. 30. 9-10, '[Alfene], tua dicta omnia factaque/ ventos irrita ferre . . . sinis;' in 64. 59, [Ariadne] irrita ventosae linquens promissa procellae,' '[promissa] quae cuncta aerii discerpunt irrita venti;' in c. 76. 8-9, '[Catulle] haec a te dicta factaque sunt. / Omnia quae ingratae perierunt credita menti.' The phrases used in c. 65 to disclaim forgetting Ortalus' request, a request 'credita gratae menti,' are those spoken elsewhere at times of real abandonment. If stated as assertion these phrases would signify the end of all relationships, whether of intellectual friendship or of physical love.

Catullus uses such charged language because for him all acts of keeping faith are highly important. (Some kind of *foedus amicitiae* existed between Catullus and Ortalus.) [1] Further, he has just mentioned the most profound act of keeping faith, 'semper amabo, semper canam,' in reference to his brother. His art will always be tinged with the sorrow of absence from life of *vita frater amabilior*. The center of c. 65 stands at 'semper amabo, semper canam,' which two activities form the core of Catullus' existence as man

---

[1] See Elder (cited page 1, note 1 above) 129.

and as poet. Keeping faith holds this center together. It is the *mens ingrata* that blights and kills. Not to violate *sancta fides* or *foedus*, not to deceive, not to leave unsaid or undone 'quaecumque homines bene cuiquam aut dicere possunt aut facere,' these are the characteristics *vitam puriter agendi*, of *pietas*, as Catullus understands it (c. 76). Hence the importance which he attaches to complying with Ortalus' and Allius' requests.

One should note that both c. 65 and *68* answer requests for poetry in neoteric style. If Lieberg is correct in interpreting *68*. 10 'munera et Musarum . . . et Veneris' as 'carmina docta et amatoria,' that is, "epyllion," then 'dulcis Musarum fetus' means neoteric poetry.[1] In both *68* and *65* it is death that forbids Catullus to comply with his friends' wishes. Just as c. 68 moves from a brief preoccupation with the love of Protesilaus and Laodamia to the poet's own love story (colored in turn by the references from myth) so c. 65, a much shorter poem (24 lines compared to 160) touches briefly upon Procne and the fate of Itylus (Itys) and then ends with a scene of a girl in love. There have already been noted further similarities between the two poems (which does not mean that explication of *68* insures success in explicating *65*). Where the rhetoric of *68* is leisurely, discursive and direct, in *65* it is compressed, symbolic and indirect. In *68* the poet's beloved makes an epiphany as a goddess in the poet's borrowed *domus* (only later to abandon him,) and her foot is singled out for specific mention (*68*. 70). In *65* the poet's brother left his *domus* only to die; his foot, the symbol of journey, as the beloved's was of critical change, is specified (*65*. 6). The critical problems of *68* are those of evaluating form and interpreting the symbolism of the characters and scenes which emerge and blend into succeeding images; in *65*, a great problem is the function of lines 19-24, the *ut* comparison clause. The metaphors of *65* are so compressed as to be legitimate symbols: one for one equivalents of deeply rooted significances in Catullus' life and his poetry.

If examined in light of what referential information they convey, the concluding six lines seem needlessly freighted with detail. If the poet intended only a simile for "something slips my mind by chance" and hit upon "like a girl's apple which lay forgotten

---

[1] Lieberg, *Puella Divina* (cited in note 2 above) 160 ff., esp. 161; see also Fraenkel (cited page 18, note 3) 262.

in her lap, and on her rising fell and rolled away," why should
the reader be informed as to the provenance of the apple, the nature
of the lap's owner, the reason for standing up, and the conscious
blush at the end? It is an important question, for the "extraneous"
material takes up about half of the six-line conclusion, or one-eighth
of the whole poem. Careful analysis of these six lines shows that
in them the poet has concentrated key words which are correlatives
to the important words of the preceding 18 lines. The last six lines
of c. 65 constitute the end of the poem, not an ending for it. For
instance, *manat ore rubor* is a conscious and skillful development
from *pallidulum manans pedem* (line 6) which looks back in turn
to *mens fluctuat*. The parallel would alone suffice to show how
crucial the long *ut* clause is to the whole import, intellectual as
well as aesthetic, of c. 65. The last six lines can be integrated.
They can be shown to be the conclusion of the text of a poem
reading as does c. 65. 1-18. Of course, the principle of metaphoric
criticism, the possibility of total poetic identification,[1] must
not be abused. Little would be gained for instance by making
all the nouns of 65 into symbolic synonyms for *frater* or *carmen*.
Yet we must be prepared to read this radical poem in a radical
way if we want to gain a sense of its artistic unity and significance.

Catullus, mindful of the duties of friendship, sends *haec carmina
expressa* to Ortalus. So the *sponsus*, one who has undertaken a
promise and pledge to continue in a certain relationship, sends
an apple to the person to whom he has made this promise. The
apple in pastoral literature is regularly a love token. The girl
in c. 65 received it from a would-be lover, and blushes at its un-
expectedly coming to view because her secret relationship is
compromised. Also, it may hint at her own seduction. *haec carmina
expressa* leads one back to *dulcis Musarum fetus*, for a *malum* is a
kind of *fetus*.[2] Hence the apple is metaphorically a gift in fulfillment
of a promise, a gift of a living thing. Catullus' poetic intellect
(*mens animi*) is presented to one who stands in the relation of
beloved to lover, that is, in the relationship of friendship as Catullus
could conceive of it. Attention has been called to the function of

---

[1] This type of criticism is perhaps developed best for modern literature
by Northrop Frye, *The Anatomy of Criticism* (Princeton, 1957).

[2] See Vergil, *Georg.* 1. 55; 2. 390. Ellis: "*fetus*, perhaps with the idea
found in Pindar that poets are the keepers of the golden apples of the Muses
(fr. 273 Bergk)."

poetry which Catullus will in future write (lines 11-12). Future
poems will grow out of his grief at the loss of his beloved brother.
Now it is with his brother that Catullus experiences the closest
relationship in c. 65. Neither Catullus and Ortalus nor *sponsus*
and *virgo* are characterized (except by refulgence) with language
as solemn as *semper amabo, semper canam*. Metaphorically the
apple is as well Catullus' tendance and love for his dead brother
(as *munere mortis, tristi munere, 101*. 3, 8; *furtivo munere malum*,
65, 19) given secretly like a stolen thing because all such gifts
fail to reach through the barrier of death, and must fall short
of their intended goal. They must "fall from the lap and roll
headlong away," as the language of 65 puts it.

Reference has already been made to Catullus' pre-occupation
in 65 with the possibility of enjoying a kind of communion with
his brother through art. The *malum missum, dulcis fetus Musarum*,
is an example of the redeeming function of poetry, for it will lie
for a brief while *molli sub veste locatum*. Although the girl will
stand up and reveal her gift and her temporary possession of it,
forgetful that it was upon her lap, Troy, 'commune sepulcrum
Asiae Europaeque,' (68. 89) will not give up its dead. Rather,
'Troia Rhoeteo quem subter litore tellus/ ereptum nostris obterit
ex oculis' (65. 7-8). Catullus' brother cannot acknowledge the
poet's gifts: 'et mutam nequiquam alloquerer cinerem' (*101*. 4).
There is ironic and poignant contrast between on the one hand the
brother dead and buried, whom no eye will see again, whom Trojan
earth crushes, whose pale limbs Lethe bathes; and on the other
the girl alive and standing up, drawing attention with her apple
which rushes forth to view. A blush suffuses her face because
she knows (*conscius*) her gift is no longer a secret, and because
she realizes she has forgotten such an important *munus*: hence
tristi miserae oblitae. Catullus' brother has passed totally into
forgetfulness; only the poet can through art briefly restore him
to the living. The girl suffers only a temporary lapse of memory,
and blood, the color of life, rushes back into her face, while even
the lowest limb of Catullus' brother is as pale in death as the waters
of Lethe that suffuse it.[1] The *virgo* has not forgotten her *sponsus*,

---

[1] In a minuscule note L. M. Kaiser, "Waves and Color in Catullus 65,"
Classical Bulletin 27 (1950) 2, adumbrates what may be a similar line of
thought. He draws attention to the apple's crimson flash and the rosy
stain on the girl's cheek. Further parallels are desirable: Ovid *Met.* 3. 484 ff.:

only his gift. Similarly, Catullus was not estranged from the Muses of neoteric love poetry forever, but represents himself as only temporarily separated from them by a death which will be the center of his forthcoming poetry. So he will redeem his brother from permanent oblivion by art as he will do for the name of Allius in c. 68.[1] Thus the separation from his brother will only be intermittent.

The *virgo* may possibly function as an idealized model for Lesbia. Catullus frequently characterises himself as the one who has kept faith; by implication, it is Lesbia who does not keep faith. If Lesbia figures at all in c. 65, she lives as the *virgo* who is, the poet hopes, only temporarily unmindful of his gift of art and life to her. As custodian of Catullus' *munus*, Lesbia is in a responsible position, just as Catullus is responsible for not forgetting Ortalus' request.

As the profanation of Procne's *domus* caused her lament and indeed gave her a changed form as perpetual lamenter, so death's profanation of Catullus' *domus* changes him. It dislodges him from the *persona* of the neoteric love poet. Female psychological processes interested Catullus; Attis and Ariadne are in certain ways aspects of Catullus' own character, and if his existence as poet centers on that of the anonymous girl of c. 65. 19-24 there should be no surprise. This *virgo* unites her momentary forgetfulness and abiding awareness of her *foedus amicitiae* in her blush. Two aspects of the poet Catullus are here set forth by c. 65. He is momentarily set apart from the young growth of the Muses (love poetry), and he is temporarily alienated by his grief from communion with his brother (love poetry written not out of convention but out of reality, out of the intermissions of the heart). Yet he is always a poet, forever aware of his love for his brother: 'semper amabo, semper canam.' Catullus the poet keeps faith with his Muses and with his friend Ortalus; if *mens animi* cannot *expromere* it can at any rate *exprimere*. It cannot fall back on a store of inner resource or spiritual energy. It can only fashion something new

---

'nudaque marmoreis percussit pectora palmis/ pectora traxerunt roseum percussa ruborem,/ non aliter quam poma solent, quae candida parte,/ parte rubent...' Hence in the apple the colors white and red are found. *Malum* in Catullus 65 is the apple, not quince or anything else, because the apple is the traditional love gift. See e.g. Propertius 1. 3. 24: 'nunc furtiva caris poma dabam manibus.'

[1] In his seriousness of intent Catullus arrogates one of the functions of the epic poet.

from common stock, and elicit art not from *Erlebnis* but *Bildung*.
Carmen 66 is the result. But the greater faith is kept, and the
promise is solemnly undertaken to sing again specifically of the
brother's death. The poet both forgets and recalls his commitments
in the specific figure of the young girl.

Critics have not noted that c. 65 is as much a poem of dedication
and promise as it is an apology and introduction for c. 66. The
correlatives *etsi* and *tamen* govern c. 65 as they did Catullus' life.
Even though he did not, as *phaselus*, encounter smooth sailing,
even though as Ariadne he was abandoned in hostile country,
as Attis by his own crazed act made an unmanned prey to madness
and despair, still he can picture an uncontaminated *domus* where a
virgo receives love gifts in purity. Catullus participates in her life
for a brief moment. The *virgo* starts up unaware of the gift con-
cealed; Catullus' poetry, his capacities for suffering, his affections
are soon revealed, however.[1] At the revelation or epiphany of his
gift, life called up by the *munus* which he had received from the
Muses and from loving Lesbia and his brother flows again through
the veins. The *munus* is nothing if not his existence as poet. He
cannot at this time bring forth his *munus* as love poet; momentarily
forgotten it rolls away. Yet it is awareness of his *munus* that
quickens him to life. Art could redeem the poet's life as well as
the poet's dead brother.

This realization, which is the result of Catullus' great powers
of abstraction and symbolizing, is obliquely revealed in 65, 19-24.
It is specifically these powers that determine the level of intent
in not only Catullus' poetry but in all poetry. Poetry in its use of
metaphor sometimes comes close to being pure metaphoric or
symbolic statement. When it does it comes closest to the center
of poetic language and participates most fully in what makes
poetry differ from other modes of discourse: the complete identification of an order of words and a non-verbal order, be it physical,
psychological or mythic. In such a statement the poet as an individual man, who lives in a world where a brother may die, a
friend may forget, or a lover may betray, becomes most fully the
artist who passes through these particularistic experiences and
transmutes them into something general and timeless, who saves

---

[1] Line 23 is a poet's line: sound's imitation of the sensory picture draws
attention to the fabric of the verse.

them from time and hence from death. Such a poet deals in symbols of universal human import.[1] These symbols arise from intuitive awareness of the processes of poetic thought, and of the nature of poetry. They are ordered according to strict economy, and their stature is enhanced by their juxtaposition one to another. The reader notices their existence first because they seem extraneous and gratuitous, and do not fit into a scheme of development rooted in rational discursiveness, which can be elicited through the rhetoric of systematic thought. The reader cannot "scan" or "parse" these symbols, not because they are esoteric and personal, half of an allegory to the other half of which he does not hold the key. Rather, they are themselves the very processes of symbolic thought. They signify themselves, nothing else. They mutually enhance and support each other without reference to other things existing outside the closed world of the poem's text. The apple is as real as the poet's brother, or his grief, or the wave of Lethe: that is, either totally poetically real and full of its own significance, or completely unreal. We may conjecture that we know that Catullus never had a brother who died, was a recluse without friends, and never knew a Lesbia save by gossip; the texts he composed would not cease to be poems of grief, friendship and love. It makes no difference which view one adopts. Everything in poetry is mimesis and hence inventive. This arrangement of symbols orders words and hence "reality."

Accordingly, in c. 65 the concluding image of the young girl resolves all that has gone before, and the preceding lines take on resonance when seen by a reader who has understood the end of c. 65. The apple of life is no longer the poet's; it has slipped away from him just as his brother has. The keeper of the apple, forgetful of it for a moment, though indubitably its possessor even as it slips away, blushes with life. So the poet will later sing his brother back into the living world where time cannot destroy art. He will become his grief like Procne, but unlike her the *domus* of his ideal will remain pure. The *sponsus* will come to give gifts to be kept *casto gremio*. Catullus will remember his *fides* with Ortalus as well as his brother, and his own hidden talent as poet who endowed

---

[1] Cf. "a set of objects, a situation, a chain of events," objective correlatives, "expressing emotion in the form of art." T. S. Eliot, "Hamlet," *Selected Essays* (London, 1957) 145.

him with *furtivum munus*, the blush of life in art, unconquered by *caeca nox*, and *fugiens aetas* (68. 42-43).

Life will come out of the death of his brother. The *dulcis Musarum fetus* will grow again as 'maesta tua carmina morte.' *Carmina Battiadae* are only temporary; the poet's gift has not rolled away forever. It has returned in 65 and will return with the strength of new growth. In the *virgo* the real death of his brother becomes symbolic rebirth; he lives on in her. In her too the poet finds liberation from his own nature and from time. In her the symbol of the red apple which is also white becomes her sympathetic blush and turns her for a moment from as it were the mother giving birth to the *fetus* into *fetus*, the apple of new growth itself. In her the images of *doctae virgines*, *fetus*, *pes pallidulus*, and *frater* coalesce and find at the same time their correlative. The *virgo*, Catullus' correlative as well, is the focus and content for this myth of death and rebirth, a subjective myth growing out from Catullus' own life into the objective world of this poem.

If poem 65 were to be analyzed to the degree of sophistication suggested by its "level of intent," it would not emerge as the pattern of symbolic discourse here suggested. Formally, c. 65 is a covering letter which excuses its writer's preoccupation with another matter and fulfills a promise made earlier. Syntactically it is of the simplest construction. Its images, such as the whirlpool of death, the song of Procne, the fallen apple, are all clear. What is momentous is the texture brought about by locking these images into a poem of this shape, a poem which moves from concession to the problematical in life to assertion of will: 'etsi me cura sevocat, tamen mitto carmen.' It is the reciprocal impact which these images have upon each other that raises them to the level of the symbolic, the poem's final significance. This poem's meaning is its configuration, as well as its discursive sense.[1]

If understood as a private poetic communication poem 30 displays a lower level of intent than 65. But if seen as a manipulation of important symbolic patterns c. 30 gains in stature and its complexities can be relatively successfully resolved. Its metaphorical utterances are part of Catullus' vocabulary, the register of expressions developed by him for giving formal expression to his

---

[1] In this way 65 is a more profound utterance than many poems to which Quinn and Putnam addressed themselves.

poetic impulses or concerns. The significance of c. 30 is to be sought in the meaning conferred by the arrangement of patterns emergent in other Catullan poems. Metaphor in c. 30 becomes symbol only because of the place which this poem takes in the community of the Catullan corpus, which enhances the arrangement of metaphors in c. 30 with other resonances of meaning. *Carmen* 50 remains the most exoteric of the three poems so far considered, and the one with a "level of intent" at least as low as c. 30. But it also strikes a metaphoric attitude, and becomes a "métaphore vécue," to coin a phrase. Considerations of great personal importance to the poet loom behind the friendly banter. Catullus was no doubt aware of the presence of these feelings, but since they neither impeded nor unduly controlled his poem's development, he did not conceal or remove them. They remain to engage the critic who is willing to see them.

It is probably not exaggeration to say that each poem of Catullus demands new critical insight, and new techniques with which to educe that poem's essential form and the nature of its latent relationships to other poems. Only the creation of new techniques enables the critic to judge the depth to which he should probe his text, and hence the extent to which the poem in question is a symbolic structure. C. 65, for example, which is a symbolic arrangement, is not only important in its own right as an exceptional poem. It can also teach the critic a good deal about the poetic process itself. Such analytical techniques provide access to Catullus' rare poetic intellect, which is perhaps at its most complex in c. 65 and *68*.

The poems of Catullus differ in many ways from those of other ancient poets. In elegists like Propertius or lyricists like Horace, the critic can discover no reason to emphasize either the verbal construction or art or the emotionally grounded communication. In the Ovid of the *Heroides* or *Amores*, the artistic fabric is often more to the fore than what the poet says. In times when techniques are perfectible, control of manner becomes increasingly valuable to a poet, and takes precedence in his poems. He can display elegant variation without renewed transfusions of experience, whether real or fictional. Also, the ascendancy of the poem's fabric makes judging easy for his audience in a time when little distinguishes one poet from another, that is, when a high degree of homogeneity in schooling and culture and taste obtains. At periods

when re-evaluation of cultural and intellectual premises is going
forward, originality is at a premium, and often it is the originality
of sense, not form, that is sought. At such times, as in the later
19th century, sincerity becomes a touchstone, and formal excellence
is not imposed by the poet or expected by his audience. In the
poems of Catullus, both situations obtain simultaneously, perhaps
because of his immediate audience, a small and accomplished
group, who were the heirs of Valerius Cato's labors. They were
skilled enough to recognize (and perhaps to expect) on the one
hand a high degree of formal excellence, and on the other a high
level of emotional sophistication expressed in their new style.
The tone and wit of a circle in which a woman and a poem were
apprehended by the same aesthetic vocabulary cannot be under-
rated.[1]

The theory of the levels of intent[2] is useful in drawing attention
to the fact that not all of Catullus' poems are of equal weight or
seriousness. But it fails to take into account that in those texts of
relatively low artistic intent there is still some level of emotional,
semantic, intent, or intention to communicate. This level may be
no lower than that in poems of greater artistic merit. There is no
poem without art, though undigested experience of a poet, or its
incipient or underdeveloped communication, can approach the
poetic before being confined in words. Similarly, there is no poem
without some communication ultimately translatable, however
poorly, into referential language. Both artistic statement and
referential statement are present in a poetic text by implication
of definition: a poem uses words but not in their ordinary non-
poetic way. There are far less useful standards for judging poems
than the degree to which they effect a balance or union between
the two factors here rather grossly isolated.

Pöschl together with critics of modern literatures has tended
to show that the art and the communication are ultimately the

---

[1] See carm. 1. 1; 6. 2; 10. 4, 33; 16. 7; 22; and many others. Also cf. the
opening of Horace *Epistles* I. 20: 'Vertumnum Ianumque, liber, spectare
videris,/ scilicet ut prostes Sosiorum pumice mundus,' etc.

[2] See above, page 1, n. 1. Quinn thinks that *68* is not fully finished (71) and
that it exhibits Catullus' "self-deception" (81) and "less personal involve-
ment" (43) than other poems. He finds *68* "rather unsatisfactory" (83).
These judgments no doubt result from his critical method, his theory of
levels of intent.

same thing.[1] For mature critical purposes, the dichotomy between form and content ceases to exist, and levels of intent can be put to work to fulfill the mandate to discuss and to evaluate. Though there may be some justice in using this critical vacuum-filler it is more appropriate as a valuable criterion and mode of discussion in some poems than in others. In *carmen* 68 the theory of levels of intent neither illuminates the complex façade of the formal structure nor reconciles to it the rich emotional progress which that structure sustains. Poem 68 contains within itself all that is needed for its explication.[2] Art and significance coincide perfectly. The presumed identity of form and content is basic to understanding *68*.

In *68*, unlike *65*, the covering letter serves to prepare for and to present the text of the poem itself. The opening 40 lines, and the concluding dozen lines, frame a text which is not to be severed from its introduction, as *66* is from *65*. Several ties unite the three parts of this text. First is the repetition of the theme of fraternal loss, precisely in the center of lines 41-148 (91-100), which also figures in the introduction, lines 19-26.[3] Second, 'mihi quam dederit duplex Amathusia curam,' line 51, loses much of its point if deprived of line 18, '[dea] quae dulcem curis miscet amaritiem.' Finally, the concluding section of the poem is intolerably irrelevant if lines 1-40 are removed; and lines 1-40, coupled with 149-160, would make an unintelligible unit without the sense of lines 41-148 after 1-40 and before 149-160.[4]

---

[1] Viktor Pöschl, *Die Dichtkunst Virgils*, (Innsbruck-Vienna, 1950.)

[2] Of much use is J. P. Elder (page 1, note 1 above) 126-131. Lieberg, (page 1, note 2 above) is occasionally helpful. For a full discussion of Lieberg's book, particularly on *68*, see the author's review in *Classical Philology* 61 (1966) 197-200. Giuseppe Pennisi, "Il carme 68 di Catullo," *Emerita* 27 (1959) 89-109, 213-238 has written the most recent perceptive discussion of this poem. He is strongly against the *chorizontes*, and his hard-headed straight thinking is most suggestive (even if he does not see the ring composition). In contrast are Luigi Pepe, "Il mito di Laodamia nel carme 68 di Catullo," *Giornale italiano di filologia* 6 (1953) 107-113, and L. Ferrero, *Interpretazione di Catullo* (Turin, 1955) 80-87.

[3] The aesthetic implication of the verbal echo will be dealt with below, p. 39.

[4] For the usual remarks counselling separation, see Fordyce (page 2, note 2 above), 341 ff. E. Fraenkel, *Gnomon* 34 (1962) 261 ff. is salutary on *68*. Perhaps the most cogent arguments for unity were assembled by Pennisi (note 2 above). Henry W. Prescott, "The Unity of Catullus lxviii," *TAPA* 71 (1940) 473-500 goes far toward eliciting the structure of prologue and

Georg Luck has said of *68*,[1] "Hier und eigentlich nur hier hat [Catull] mit kühnen Griff der mythischen Welt ein Gegenbild für seine persönliche Erfahrung entnommen . . . Für Properz und Ovid ist der Mythos eine selbstverständliche Form Erlebtes aufzufassen und darzustellen." Yet this poem of personal statement is in a highly normative form, the omphalos structure. The other three poems of Catullus discussed here have depended in various ways upon metaphor and symbol in order to communicate meaning and to constitute art. Poem 68 however is neither more open in its statements, like *50*, nor more tied to esoteric, private usage of image and language, like *30*. But it is difficult to understand as a poetic construction in which seemingly disparate or irrelevant elements are to be referred to an overarching concept cr pattern of words. Poem 68 depends for its unification upon a formal structure, which has been discussed with varying degrees of perception by commentators and critics. For Kroll, it is "alexandrinische Spielerei;" for Luck, "sorgfältig ausgewogenen Ordnung." [2] Kroll observed glimmers of the fire of strong feeling through this structure's chinks, and for him this poetic glow is what makes the *Spielerei* bearable. L. Richardson's[3] and C. Whitman's[4] techniques and principles are predicated upon other grounds. Accordingly they do not justify formal ordering with intimations of biography.

Luck does not ask what the omphalos construction[5] contributes to or takes away from the poet's symbolizing powers as exhibited in *68*. In other poems such as those discussed in this paper Catullus relies upon language and its ordering powers to build up a texture of emotional implication and release. In *68*, language itself is built into an order, or a structure which is basically non-verbal. It is intelligible as a rationally excogitated hierarchy of values assigned to the themes of the poem. The length and the disposition of the poem's sections constitute a statement. A brief study of the diagram of *68* (derived in large part from Luck) [6] shows that the heart

epilogue embracing a unit, 41-148: see pp. 477, 488. Lenchantin de Gubernatis finally came out for two poems: *Catullo, Carmina Selecta* (Turin, 1950) 123-124.

[1] Georg Luck, *Die römische Liebeselegie* (Heidelberg, 1961) 61.

[2] Luck, *Liebeselegie* 59.

[3] L. Richardson, *Poetical Theory in Republican Rome* (New Haven, 1944).

[4] C. Whitman, *Homer and the Heroic Tradition* (Cambridge, Mass., 1958).

[5] See diagram, and page 31, note 1 below.

[6] Note 1 above. The German edition corrects and amplifies his *The Latin Love Elegy* (London 1959) 50 ff.

of *68* is the dead brother of the poet. Troy surrounds him on two literal levels: he is buried in Trojan soil and he is buried in the middle of a poem which uses Trojan characters. The central section about the brother, 91-100, is bracketed on either side by Paris and Helen (87-90; 101-104). Thus the poem's literal and figurative center is the poet's brother.

	1-40	introduction
10 lines	41-50	*foedus* of Allius and Catullus
6	51-56	Catullus' own love: torture of desire
16 (=13+3)	57-72	Allius' relief compared: epiphany of the *diva*
14	73-86	Laodamia and Protesilaus
2	87-88	Helen
2	89-90	Troy: tomb
10	91-100	dead brother
2	101-102	Greek youth: hearth
2	103-104	Paris
14	105-118	Laodamia and Protesilaus
16 (=13+3)	119-134	Laodamia's love compared: epiphany of the *diva*
6	135-140	Catullus' own love: torture of self
10*	141-148	*foedus* of Catullus and his mistress
	149-160	conclusion

Diagram of poem 68

Catullus is an unusual poet. What has been suggested about the ending of *65* suffices to show the critic that he deals with a poet of immense imaginative resource. In the organization of *68* Catullus has created a structural, mensurable model of a metaphor. The omphalos structure of *68* is not a framework upon which the poet rests his elements of sentiment and thought, that is, the metaphoric epidermis. Rather, the structure of *68*, the central mass of which runs from lines 41 to 148, constitutes yet another register upon which the poet works. Meaning is literally imbedded in form, inseparable and itself conditioned by and communicated through its placement.

The "recessed panel" technique, or ring composition,[1] is not

---

* For this number see G. Luck, *Die römische Liebeselegie* (Heidelberg, 1961) 59-60.

[1] W. A. A. van Otterlo, "Untersuchungen über Begriff, Anwendung, u. Entstehung der griechischen Ringkomposition," *Med. der Ned. Akad. van Wetenschappen*, Afd. Letterkunde, N. R. D. 7, No. 3 (Amsterdam 1944): "Eine merkwürdige Kompositionsform der älteren griechischen Literatur," *Mnemosyne* 12 (ser. 3) (1944), 192-207. Henri Bardon, *L'art de la composition chez Catulle*, Publications de l'université de Poitiers, Série "Sciences de l'homme" III (Paris 1943) regards "68-68a" as exhibiting the *embrassé* structure rather than the enumerative (45 f.). In drawing attention to

utilized here for the same reasons as led to relying upon it in oral compositions. In oral poetry the form of narration depends upon the objective circumstances of the performance. In brief, the poet composing orally finds it convenient to adopt a reversing order when enumerating or recapitulating enumerated items in a series. For Catullus, the criterion was not convenience of composition but rather the aesthetic expectations of his audience. Alexandrianism recognized the Homeric organization's framework, and used it with the composition of relatively long poems, so-called "epyllia." This device contributed to Alexandrian critics' idea of what such a poem should look like.

In poem 64, Catullus uses a ring composition of more spacious dimensions than in 68. In 64, he applies ring composition not only to the whole poem (*grosso modo*, wedding scene—coverlet—wedding scene) but also to each segment. For instance, the song of the Parcae begins with a consideration of the scene before their eyes (328 ff.) and after touching upon Achilles' career, it returns to the wedding night (372 ff.). This may rightly be called *Spielerei*: its non-aesthetic ethos or justifying function is not tragic or even personal. It is ostensibly playful in a child-like way. For what links Ariadne's lament, the centerpiece of 64, to its frame is its own center, line 163 (the lament proper runs from 132 to 201, 71 lines): 'purpureave tuum consternens veste cubile.' If the poet had stopped to examine that coverlet, no doubt it would resemble that of 49 ('tincta roseo conchyli purpura fuco') and of 265 ('vestis decorata figuris'), the immediate lines constituting the frame. Here Catullus makes unity out of circumstantial similarities, namely, the coverlet and coverlet descriptions. The external structure of 64 cohesively presents an internal construction which is not tragic, as 68 may be said to be. Catullus in 64 has constructed a *persona* which is basically ironic in its obtuseness in positing a high point of morality in the days when gods and mortals were each other's guests, when Ariadne could be abandoned and Achilles killed many in a war over an adulterous woman. The poem is completely comprehensible without attributing to the narrator-poet any unique position in reference to his subject. However, in 64

Catullus' independence of Greek models, he cogently observes, "dans l'ordre embrassé comme dans l'ordre énumératif, c'est sur sa vie intérieure que Catulle modèle sa technique et sa dette envers un Callimaque est infime." (69). If an overstatement, it is largely true.

Catullus presents a judgment of his theme by making it work with a superabundance of Alexandrian links and ties, balances and figures, behind which he ironically precipitates an ethical evaluation of his material. In *64* he creates the recessed panel construction, but his *persona* achieves a distance from it. That distance is irony.

In *68*, the omphalos or ring composition is again put into service of the *persona*. But in *68*, as will emerge more fully in subsequent discussion, there is no distance, whether aesthetic, ethical or ironic, between poet and structure. Rather, Catullus in *68* makes the structural pattern into a model of his own psychological state as he represents himself composing the poem. Catullus metaphorically becomes *68* in structure, just as he draws its themes from his own preoccupations.

Contrast with *65* and *66* is instructive. In *65* the poet's mind 'fluctuat tantis malis' (4) that he cannot *expromere* the sweet fruits of the Muses (3). Nevertheless he is able to send *expressa carmina Battiadae*. In c. *68*, the poet says, 'accipe quis merser fortunae fluctibus ipse' (13) which reminds one of the images of fluidity which Catullus used in *65*. *Carmen 66* is more or less translation from Callimachus. *Carmen* 68. 41-148 is Alexandrian "epyllion" in form. How much does the *scriptorum non magna copia*, the *una ex multis capsula* (33, 36) account for the shape of c. 68. 41-148? The question is important, for *68* is obviously not translation, but a new kind of poetry, which, as it were, wears the shape of a public narrational poem in modern style, but embodies personal concerns partly set forth in terms of myth. Poem 68 is not the *munus* which Allius[1] has asked for as 'munera et Musarum et Veneris.' It is no lament of Ariadne, as in *64*, nor a "Lock of Berenice," as *66*. Allius has not got what he asked for because Catullus has only a small supply of poets' works with him. Evidently Allius wanted a neoteric "epyllion" which in some way depended upon earlier poems. What he got was a poem of impeccable Alexandrian structure, a perfect ring composition, but one which presents a highly individualistic theme or series of themes.

---

[1] Allius is used here of the person addressed throughout the poem in place of the cumbersome Malius, Manlius or Allius. For the problem of the name see Fraenkel (page 29, note 4 above) with whom I am in agreement, 262; Pennisi (page 29, note 2 above) 228-36. Likewise Lesbia can be used of the *candida diva* for convenience. Catullus chose not to mention his beloved's name in order to make her consistently the perfected *diva*, unflawed and universal. Her human personality intrudes at lines 135 ff., however.

The carefully controlled public structure holds the private themes in balance, inasmuch as the structural pattern is largely thematic. The tension of a poem built in this way is unmistakable. The poet asserts at the outset, 'nequeo,' "I am unable to comply with your friendly request for song." This is linked to the opening of the high-style section, 'non possum,' "I am unable to keep silent about Allius' good offices (because Allius gave me scope and ground for poetry)." Ambiguity and paradox are increased by conjoining the poet's greatest moment of joy, the epiphany of his beloved as a goddess, to his greatest sorrow, the death of his brother. Real and mythical, Allius and Hercules, *puella* and Protesilaus, succeed each other and unfold to manifest the poet's brother, dead in Troy.

Carmen 68 is more complex than 65 not only because of its three movements (1-40; 41-148; 149-160) but because the *mens animi* of Catullus in 68 does not end in pure metaphor like the *virgo* of 65. He achieves a more far-reaching metaphor which is personal expression interpenetrated and interpreted by mythological figures. Here, Catullus makes verse structure into not merely an orderly exposition of these expressions but also a complex statement in its own right.

Mention has already been made of the ambiguity of this poem's *nequeo* and *non possum*, which link the opening movement and the principal section of the text. Other significant links are the following. In line 12, *hospitis officium* occurs.[1] In line 42, *quantis [Allius] iuverit officiis*, the noun has become Allius' performance of an office of friendship. Further, the word occurs a third time in the coda of the poem, line 150, *munus pro multis, Alli, officiis*, where again it signifies what Allius did for Catullus. These opening lines of the conclusion offer other parallels besides *officiis*, a key word for this poem. *Quod potui*,[2] line 149, looks back to *non possum*, 41, and *nequeo*, 32, already mentioned. *munus*, 149, and *munera*, 154, echo *munera* in 10 and 32, and seem to refer to the gift which the addressee solicited from the poet, and which the poet sent to his friend.[3] The fact that the word occurs four times shows its

---

[1] Lieberg (page 1, note 2 above) 156 takes *hospitis* as objective genitive, the duty owed to a host.

[2] *quod potui* is important not least as the first line of the third section. Kroll saw it as crucial for unifying the text.

[3] On *munus* see Lieberg (page 1, note 2 above) 157 f.; Pennisi (page 29, note 2 above) esp. 108.

importance: this is a poem of offering and of giving. There are other verbal parallels in the three segments of *68*. In the covering letter, *hoc studium*, 19, in reference to love's preoccupations, and *haec studia*, 26, represent *gaudia* and *deliciae animi* in general. In line 44, *studium* is used of Allius' *officium* performed for Catullus. The word *aetas* is employed three times. First, Catullus uses it to name the time of his life when he loved, *florida aetas*, line 16. Its second occurrence refers to the same thing: *Romae carpitur aetas*. It makes a third appearance in the main body of the text as *fugiens aetas*, 43; there Catullus can feel the rush of forgetful ages (and his own passing) and wants to keep Allius' *studium* fresh. The verb *lusi* occurs twice, in line 17, to characterize the poet's love-filled youth and (as Fordyce neglects to mention) [1] the erotic poetry he then composed. The second appearance is at line 156, *lusimus*, where the sense is surely the same as *exerceremus amores* of line 68. From the point of view of *68*, the time of love seems to belong to the past, except for the concluding lines. Finally, *domus* occurs twice, as may be expected in a poem which proffers thanks for a friend's kind loan of a house: lines 34, where the poet says his own *domus* is in Rome; and 156, where he hopes that the *domus* of Allius, together with its *domina*, will prosper.

From the foregoing parallels it should be easier to see that poem 68 is a whole text which ostensibly centers upon *officium, munus*, and the poet's inability, which becomes ability, to perform his own *officium* and to make his own *munus* in return for *officium perfectum*. The *officium* bestowed upon him by his friend was to provide scope for *ludere*, in an *aetas* when the poet was not impeded from loving and writing poetry. At the moment when Allius is undone by love (it need not be as serious as Fordyce [p. 343], makes out: lines 27 ff. can be frivolous in tone), Catullus cannot write neoteric poetry based on present involvements, or learned poetry like *64* or *66*, because of his own grief. It is a bereavement of the heart, not the loss of his beloved mistress, but of his beloved brother.

Discursive description of the epidermis of this text does not afford much help in coming to an understanding of its formal structure, its excursions into myth, or the relationship between

---

[1] See Quinn (page 1, note 1 above) 108 note 15; and page 5, note 1 above.

form and statement. In a discussion of the central process of *68*,
lines 41-148, a survey of recurring motifs is as useful as a survey
of recurring words. The most frequently recurring topic is that
of heat: physical heat and the fires of love coalesce: *torruerit*,
line 52; *ardorem*, 53; *sudore*, 61; *aestus, exustos agros, hiulcat*, 62;
aestus again, 108; *flagrans amore*, 73; *flagrantem iram*, 139. In
contrast to heat and burning is *lympha*, 54; *fletu*, 55; *imbre madere*,
56; *rivus*, 58; *lenius aspirans aura*, 64; *emulsa palude*, 110. The
dulce levamen comes *vertice montis*, 57, *prona praeceps valle*, 59,
where it is accessible *viatori lasso*, 61. Other images of depth
include the *aestus amoris* which swept Laodamia downwards
in *abruptum barathrum* in *montis medullis* (108 and 111). Yet her
altus amor was *altior illo barathro*, 116. The contrast between fire
and cool water is paralleled by that between heights, the source
of moisture, and depths, its grounding: love, and its exit-channel:
barathrum or death and hell. A minor set of contrasts may be seen
in the whiteness associated with the coming of the beloved (*fulgentem plantam*, 71; *candida*, 70; *fulgebat*, 134; *candidus*, ibid.,)
and the redness of the blood which Laodamia omitted to shed,
thus causing her abbreviated bridal state (*sanguine*, 75; *cruorem*,
79.)

In connection with this last citation, it has been noticed that
Catullus indulges in a singular personification in 'quam ieiuna
pium desiderat ara cruorem' (line 79).[1] This personification can
be more readily assimilated to the poem if one recalls how the
viator yearns for drink a dozen and a half lines earlier. The refreshment which Allius gave to Catullus, the *dulce levamen*, would have
secured some of those long winter's nights for Laodamia, had she
not withheld it from the altar which craved it and which was
bound to Laodamia's life by some unspecified *foedus* of marriage-
rite. The *hostia* had not pacified *caelestis eros* (76) and consequently
Laodamia lost her husband by not keeping her pact with those *eri*.
(Hercules, one notes, served his *erus*, though superior to him.)

The beloved keeping faith appears before Catullus who becomes
the *vir flavus* in the marriage attended by Cupid, 130 ff. The
rara furta of his *era* (136) are both her relations with her husband,
and whatever other lapses of which Catullus may be acutely or
dimly aware. The poet will not be *molestus* about these, however

---

[1] Lieberg (page 1, note 2, above) 221 note 207.

(137); this does not signify "fussy" (Fordyce) but means, "Let me not ask too much, like a fool." That Catullus is the *vir* in his own eyes is evident from the comparison with Juno, which is another instance of the poet's preoccupation with an androgynous persona: he is Juno, his beloved is Jupiter; the *mulier* is *multivola*, the god *omnivolus* (128 and 140). One might also suggest that Catullus sees in Laodamia a kind of Ariadne, abandoned too soon after her *nox mira*.[1]

If Catullus and his *era*[2] are in some way enjoying a marriage union which is denied to Laodamia and Protesilaus it is because Catullus as *viator* had received the nourishing refreshment of the mountain spring as it flows into the valley. That is to say, in the public language of the poem, Catullus has been endowed by Allius with a place of assignation. Laodamia and Protesilaus, on the other hand, are not enjoying a similar relationship because a crucially important drink was withheld from the thirsty altar.

Without the reference to Laodamia, the import of *dulce levamen* is clear enough; it means Allius' house.[3] With the inclusion of the myth, however, its meaning becomes more complex. It remains Allius' house, to be sure, but becomes as well his friendship, the *foedus amicitiae* which united the two men, and which enabled the poet to unite with his *era*. Thus seen, the *levamen* metaphorically becomes Lesbia herself. Laodamia is not the beloved burning with love; she is love which burns but which neglects the formalities required of highly important relationships. Eager for Protesilaus, she loses him in an access of passion which inhibits her from performing *officium* due the gods. Allius, on the other hand, did not omit any particular in his *foedus* with Catullus, and the poet, by composing *68*, omits nothing on his own part. One wonders what

---

[1] Lieberg (page 1, note 2, above) advances the idea that Lesbia is Laodamia. He does not follow this up by making Catullus into Protesilaus. Catullus may share aspects of Protesilaus. Both lost women they loved, and both are overcome by a death in Troy. However, it is preferable to regard Laodamia as metaphorically the *foedus amicitiae*.

[2] *era* in line 136; it is probably better to regard *domina* of line 68 and 156 as some woman other than the poet's mistress; see Fordyce *ad loc.*, but note that *era* is not "precisely similar" to *domina*; *era* is the word used by a servant in reference to his mistress. The distance established between Catullus and his *era* is "precisely similar" to that between Laodamia and the *eri caelestes*.

[3] The punctuation of Mynors, OCT, is followed; otherwise it would seem possible to see the poet's refreshment in his own tears.

deficiency Lesbia brought to her love-relationship with Catullus.
What appears to be an ironic comparison, that is, an allusion to
Laodamia in a scene of all but nuptial bliss, is most apposite.
Laodamia is constant to one thing, her passion. She is one aspect
of a *foedus sanctae amicitiae aeternum* (*carmen* 109), namely, *studium*.
She brings no *munus* of generosity for her *eri*. Though her happiness
was great, it was brief. It was ended by her husband going to
Troy.[1]

What Catullus stresses about Laodamia is her great eagerness
for her *vir* and for her fulfillment in his embrace: 'tu . . . magnos
vicisti . . . furores,/ ut semel es flavo conciliata viro' (129-130).
That is the picture of Laodamia which the poet leaves with the
reader at the end of her second appearance. To be sure, at the
conclusion of her first appearance, Catullus brings out her loss,
abrupto coniugio (line 84), but this is not the dominant characteristic
of her figure. Laodamia is a cardinal personage in this text. She
functions in it as a comparison to Lesbia's bridal advent and serves
as a negative *exemplum* of what the poet would avoid undertaking
(77-78). After the passage moving from Paris and Helen to the
frater, and back to Paris and Helen, she re-emerges as a woman
who sustained loss in her great love for Protesilaus. For Laodamia
too, love was *duplex*. In her career in 68, Laodamia passes from
radiant joy to sorrow, and from sorrow to joy. In the movement
of this emotional process is impacted *frater ademptus*. His absence
is a constant sorrow at the heart of 68. Protesilaus left Laodamia
and *penetralis focos* (102) so that Paris' adulterous love would come
to nothing. Protesilaus' death ends two relationships: his own to
his wife, and, through his colleagues, the *lecta pubes graeca*, that
of Paris and Helen. The death of Catullus' brother likewise signals
the poet's estrangement from two relationships: *et musae et Venus*.
Death and the consequent absence of love stand at the center
of the poem and of the poet's consciousness.

One may plausibly postulate a logical excursive train of thought
for this poem. It might look like this: Catullus, in thanking Allius,
calls to mind his great relief which Allius' boon conferred: his
beloved approaching as if to her bridal. His relief and the passion

---

[1] On Lesbia's conscious defect, shown by her pausing wantonly on the
threshold, flouting both marriage and luck, see Sheldon Baker, "Lesbia's
Foot," *CP* 55 (1960) 171-173. Was Protesilaus entirely married to Laodamia
if certain obviously crucial sacrifices were not performed?

of the *puella divina* coalesce in the figure of Laodamia who is
constant in her passion but flawed in her love by omission of part
of a compact, and hence undone by a death not her own. Her sad
part in the Trojan myth leads the poet on to Troy itself, where
his brother and Laodamia's husband met death. At least such a
postulated train of thought induces the critic more readily to
consider the text of *68* as a process rather than as a description
of a static state. Catullus is nowhere less a poet of *ecphrasis*, even
psychic or psychological *ecphrasis*, than in *68*. However, the
expression "train of thought" implies something adventitious or
uncontrolled. There can be little doubt that Catullus here has
cultivated that impression. But the poet has achieved a monumental
balance through omphalos technique. Such a composition as *68*.
41-148 does not result from following trains of thought. The poem
is process, to be sure. Further, it itself is symbol of the meaning
of that process. The rest of this paper will attempt to assess that
meaning and the success of the poet's technique.

The repeated passages, lines 22 ff., and 94 ff., have an aesthetic
as well as a psychological function. At their first appearance,
it is evident that the poet's brother's death has destroyed Catullus'
commoda (21), chief of which was erotic sport and the poetry
to which it gave rise. The poet's household is buried with the
brother, and the joys which their relationship sustained are past.
This statement is made within the context of the relaxed, urbane,
gentlemanly tone dominant in the poem's opening lines, and the
statement is fully consonant with its matrix. When the audience
hears these same lines repeated later, they have taken on new
significance. It is then evident what *domus* was lost, what *gaudia*,
and what *amor*. The *domus*, which the poet has emphasized as
being in Rome, was not the physical household which at the
opening of *68* one might have imagined the poet sharing with his
brother. The *domus* was the house the loan of which occasions
Catullus to speak to Allius even in sorrow. It was a house to which
a *domina* came like a goddess in order to love the poet. The *domus*
of myth to which the borrowed *domus* is compared ended because
of a deficiency in the *foedus* with the over-ruling gods. That deficiency led to one member of the *foedus* going to Troy to end a
wrongful love union. That union too was ended, but at the price
of death. Death also overtook the poet's brother in Troy, and
Catullus' unusually close relationship with him, an affinity of

blood as fervent and binding as one of passion, died too.[1] Like
Laodamia the poet survived and in images of rebirth (reminiscent
of the girl and the apple in 65) he rounds out his poem. Again,
as in 65, there is *furtivum munus* (cf. line 145). This *munus, confectum carmine*, again is given to a friend. And again, Catullus
selects images of growth, *carum confecto aetate parenti caput nepotis
seri* (119); 'a quo sunt primo omnia nata bona' (158), and the
tranquil present tense and life-affirming quality of the poem's
final line: 'lux mea, qua viva vivere dulce mihi est.'

Perhaps Catullus feared that the physical *domus* at Rome
shared with Lesbia and typified by the "house of the *mira nox*"
would end with the undoing of the spiritual *domus* shared with
his brother. Or perhaps there is no causative link between the two,
but only an associative connection, loose and unspecific. Catullus
seems only to imply that Laodamia's situation is not unlike the
one in which he finds himself. If the reading of the poem offered
here is correct, and Laodamia is in some way symbol for the
inherently flawed relationship between poet and *era*, then the
death of the brother is only a tragic parallel. It is the reality
behind the myth which serves as comparison for another objective
situation, namely the poet's possession of Lesbia *apud Allium*.
The flaw in the relationship would appear to be what the poet
tries not to be *molestus* about in 137, and which he reminds himself
of in 143 ff. She is not his wife 'sed furtiva dedit mira munuscula
nocte' (145).

In 68 Catullus has so intertwined the themes of himself and his
candida diva, Laodamia and Protesilaus, Paris and Helen, Hercules
and the dead brother, that it is impossible to separate them,
and even unwise to attempt to filter the sets of responsibilities
and emotional connections from one another. The poet makes
assertions about each of these strands of personal identity by means
of the others. What is important, and easily lost to sight, is the
fact that this poem is not only about one *nox mira* (145) but about
the relationship which that marked or initiated. Day follows
night (148) and lives are lived out together (160). The brother,
dead and buried, occupies the central place in text and mind.

---

[1] See above, pp. 17 f. on poem 65. Evidence of a fraternal epitaph has been
confronted with *68*. 94 ff. by Ignazio Cazzaniga, "Catullo B 68, 50-60 e i
vv. 1-7 del papiro Lond. di Partenio di Nicea," *Parola del Passato* 77 (1961)
124-126.

He does not, however, displace Lesbia or disqualify the poet from loving her or from carrying out the duties of friendship owed to others, as to Allius.[1]

The poet's dead brother is not inert or static. His is the controlling figure in the text. Preparation for it has been made in lines 22 ff. The first segment of the omphalos has led up to it. It is essential to consider what the complexion of the poem is up to the central panel. The poet appears saddened by *duplex Amathusia*, burned by love's heat, which is ostensibly passion, and covertly, fraternal affection as well, and he is weeping copiously (51 ff.). The site of Hercules' death, Mount Oeta, is mentioned (54), and the poet's eyes are said to be wasting away (55 ff.). These images of death and longing are continued in the story of Laodamia and in the reference to Nemesis (77), and particularized by 'Troia (nefas!) commune sepulcrum, . . . acerba cinis' (89-90). The dead brother has in anticipation colored the imagery of this first half of the poem. However, once his section is reached, read, and passed beyond, one notes a perceptible shift in the choice of images toward those conveying life. More positive elements are selected for inclusion. The Greek youth are said *deseruisse focos*; Paris is assigned *gavisus*. Although it is a negative clause of purpose, still, the aspect is positive and life-enhancing: *libera otia in pacato thalamo*. Laodamia in her downfall is addressed as *pulcherrima*; a positive side of her *coniugium* is presented: *vita dulcius atque anima*. The depth of her despair in love is likened to the drainage canal which serves to make cultivatable the *pingue solum* near Pheneus, which otherwise would be flooded by the Olbius. Again the positive is emphasized.

This passage is emphatically not "a whimsically precious mythological excursus" (Fordyce) even if it is done "in gesuchter und gelehrter Weise" (Kroll). Catullus' continuing to address himself to the *barathrum* and its supposed builder is not captious display of learning. Hercules went into the depths of the mountain to

---

[1] Note that these last two references are to the last lines of the main part of the poem and of the whole text, respectively. Pennisi (page 29, note 2 above) suggests that Catullus performs that duty in two ways. He offers his friend, whose mistress has withdrawn, an example of love's constancy even when one of the lovers is no more (Laodamia) (219). And he gives an example which handles these love-miseries in an urbane way ('ne nimium simus stultorum more molesti') which counts only the joys and does not ask too much of life ('quare id satis est . . .' 147 f.) (222).

achieve something that gives life. His function as *soter* is obvious. He was himself an ambiguous figure, 'falsiparens Amphitryoniades,' and his deed, draining off water so that crops could grow, is also ambiguous. He did away with an excess of something necessary for growth. He did this when in his more straight-forward role he obeyed a *deterior erus* and killed those monstrous man-eaters, the Stymphalian birds. He achieved divine status, everlasting life, and a divine bride. Hercules here is in his way as dominant a figure as Laodamia. Hercules the wanderer gains the center of the mountain in order both to confer life and to attain it for himself and ultimately win a bride. Catullus brings a gift to Allius which changes him (he is no longer sad and alone at the end of the poem), and plumbs the depths of sorrow to sing of the death of his brother. The poet also attains the highest experience of love with the *candida diva*. He is thus fully analogous to Hercules the benefactor, resuscitator of life and ravisher of a divine bride.

If it is upon the life-bringing aspect of Hercules that Catullus relies to begin the upward lift of this poem from the grave of his brother toward the light and life of the ending, he does not let Hercules carry that burden alone.[1] He is succeeded by another of Catullus' seemingly ingenuous paradoxical contrasts, a baby whose birth rejoices his aged grandfather, and who, an infant Hercules, drives the vulture that is like a Stymphalian bird from his grandfather's head (119 ff.).

The child who revivifies hope and sustains it is followed by a figure drawn from the world of nature: the dove which rejoices in her mate. It is characteristic of Catullus that the vignette drawn from human life makes a point about natural familial love between persons related by affinity, contrasted to birds of prey, the waiting and frustrated heirs. The imagery drawn from the animal world, the world of birds, is colored with human traits. The female dove is conceived of as taking conscious pleasure (*gavisa est*) in her mate's affectionate attentions (cf. *Paris gavisus*, 103). The mate is snowy (*niveo columbo*, 125) like the beloved woman (*candida*, 70) and Cupid (*candidus*, 134). A moral category is set up to which their love-play is referred (*improbius*, 126) and which is linked to the human world: *quam mulier quae multivola est*

---

[1] Hercules at the outset is also colored by death; he is referred to first in *68* by mention of his death place, Mt. Oeta.

(128). Laodamia is last seen in the arms of Protesilaus immediately after the passages presenting the comparisons of the lateborn child and the uninhibited doves. ' . . . tu horum magnos vicisti sola furores' (129).

It is noteworthy that *furores*, love's passion, is used both of the doves in their physical love and of the family's expression of affection for the *serus nepos*. Catullus has elsewhere made a startling assertion about the quality of his love when he wrote of Lesbia, 'dilexi . . . te pater ut gnatos diligit et generos' c. 72. 4).[1] For Catullus, the passionate depths of love were not only those of physical passion but also the love by which he was bound through a *foedus* of blood or its close associate, *amicitia*.[2] Hence Catullus can appositely compare Laodamia's passionate love for Protesilaus to doves, and to a family's joy at a new-born son, though less cogently according to modern views, particularly in light of the irony of Protesilaus' death.

Nowhere after the central panel is Protesilaus' death or Laodamia's sorrow brought up, except immediately at the re-initiation of her story, 105 f., where only *casus* and *coniugium ereptum* are used, and where it is her beauty, not her sorrow, that is particularized. Rather, Laodamia in Protesilaus' arms, beginning her marriage, is the audience's final view of her. It is important to recognize the shift in time dynamics that occurs in and around the central panel of *68*. From the present moment of Allius' help, the poet shifts to the geographical remoteness of Aetna, paralleled by Oeta, the site of Hercules' burning pyre, and back to the advent of the *domina*. She is evidently assimilated into a world remote also in time: the *quondam* of 75 reveals as much. The poet breaks the illusion of distance, however, in his prayer to *Ramnusia virgo*, 77 f., but instantly resumes, not the Lesbia scene, but the Laodamia scene which the *domina* conjured up. Time figures in a new way when Catullus calls up the succeeding winters and their long nights, which Laodamia and her *vir* did not have, and in which they might have taken a full measure of love. Those happy nights did not ensue because of the bridegroom's sudden departure, 'quod scibant Parcae non longo tempore abesse' (85). Troy appears in a double time aspect, not only a lure for Greek heroes but also

---

[1] E. Havelock, *The Lyric Genius of Catullus* (Oxford 1939) 148; Elder, (page 1, note 1 above) 128.

[2] R. Reitzenstein (page 9, note 2 above), 4-12, 15 ff.

their common tomb and the sepulchre of countless men since their day. Catullus situates Troy in an ambiguous time-dimension. It is where Protesilaus will die, and where his brother is already dead.

The dead brother is the still point in the turning of time. After his central place is reached, time resumes a course, not onward but backward. The Greeks are said to have abandoned home for principle: Laodamia's *coniugium* is indeed *ereptum* (106 f.). She is whirled *in abruptum barathrum* (108 f.; cf. *abrupto coniugio*, 84.) This is the same time-point as *docta est amisso viro* (80). After the Hercules passage, Laodamia is next encountered being taught to bear the yoke of marriage. When she next emerges, after the *serus nepos* and the *columba*, she is depicted as surpassing these examples in love as her husband takes her to himself. Time has turned back to the point where Laodamia is first introduced: 'flagrans advenit amore/ Protesileam Laudamia domum' (73 f.). Not only is there a static balance of figures around the central panel of the dead brother. There is as well a dynamic ordering of time. For Laodamia it is: coming to Protesilaus; loss of him; brother and his frame; loss of Protesilaus; learning to endure marriage; coming to Protesilaus in great passion. Preoccupation with and foreboding of death in the first half of 41-148 (e.g. Oeta, *fletu, tristi imbre, amisso viro*) give way to birth and life (*pingue solum, serus nepos unius natae*, the apparition of Cupid *crocina in tunica, dies lapide candidiore, lux mea*). So too Laodamia's story runs back upon itself and she is left happy, caught in the ordering words of this poem's world.

It appears that the poet did not care to present a specific point in time any further advanced than that presented by the center of the poem. He himself appears at the outset of the main part of *68* rejoicing in his beloved's coming to him when he was tired and burning with love. Her advent, or more specifically, Allius' bringing about her coming, which is metaphorically identical, refreshes him after heat, and calms and directs him after storm. At 131 ff., the scene is resumed without evidence of a break. She has arrived at the threshold (71) and throws herself into Catullus' embrace (131 ff.). If one sets aside the careful formal arrangement of *68*, the poem is indeed a love-poem about Catullus and his mistress. It presents his joy, his characteristic examination of his own state of mind (135 ff.), and exculpation of his beloved

(143 f.). But taking the ring composition into account obviates this one-sided view. The poet's brother is central to *68* in many ways.

It is essential to set up a unified theory to which the various themes of *68*. 41-148 may be referred. The poem, like others of Catullus' more complex and ambiguous efforts, functions simultaneously on several levels. 1. It thanks Allius by providing him with a polished poem in omphalos technique, and of Alexandrian fineness in its structure and its use of mythology. 2. It hymns the *domina* as she comes to spend *nox mira* with the poet, and also reveals the poet's own rapture at her advent. 3. It comes to terms with the poet's dead brother, and poises him at the center or on the pinnacle of the poem. 4. The poem is a movement from life through death and back to life.

The last three aspects of the text bear inquiry. The *candida diva* (behind whom Allius' gift is ever present) gives the poet a requisite of life. She is his refreshment and his life. Love and life blend together, just as does the human woman and the divine figure, *candida diva*. Thus, the second and fourth aspects are closely related. Love for Lesbia is the force which makes the poet rejoice. Love for his brother is what makes him sad. Love is indeed *duplex* in a way different from line 51 in light of line 18.[1] Love for Lesbia quickens. Love for the dead brother brings pain because he is insensible to that love. Love for Lesbia prevails. There is no question here of a contest between the living woman and the dead man for Catullus' affections. Catullus is in no way impeded from fully loving the *diva*, even though as his thoughts swing away from her they are attracted by the powerful lodestone of Troy, a lost brother and death. His passage of thought from 73 to 130 takes in psychologically mensurable time only as long as it takes the *domina* to enter the room and embrace Catullus. Insofar as this poem is a description in words of an objective event, in which Allius may be assumed, on account of his style of life, to take some appreciative interest, a long part of the text, 73-130, is extraneous. Some commentators have expressed impatience and harshness at this. But once it is observed that the poem is not only representation of an outward event but also a presentation of a psychological

---

[1] See above, p. 29.

process accompanying the outward event, objections to details
in the text can be resolved.

It is futile to wonder whether Catullus first wished to compose
an omphalos-ordered text which Allius might have been expecting,
and then saw its formal structure as a model for a psychological
state. Likewise one cannot tell whether or not the poet used the
ring composition chiefly because it offered possibilities for such a
model. Moreover, it would be imprudent to assert with confidence
that Catullus in composing 68 fully worked out the implications
set forth here. Nonetheless, these suggested interpretations bring
clarity and unity to the text. The question of whether or not the
poet intentionally makes such an inter-referential nexus of images
is difficult, for it comes close to the intentional fallacy. The point
of such a reading of this poem's movement is not to save Catullus
from the blame of commentators like Fordyce but to make more
perceptible the Catullus of sensitive critics such as Elder.[1] Before
examining the unconscious aspects of Catullus which Elder has
indicated, one should free the ordering properties of the words
which this text controls.

In the structural elements which are the armature of 68, Catullus
exposes to view what a great loss he has suffered through his
brother's death which is always somewhere in his mind. Even
at the outset of the *mira nox* consciousness of this death is either
actual, or implicit in the retrospective viewpoint of 68. But it
does not impede him from loving his mistress as the *diva* merited.
His brother's death is strongly enough felt to keep him from
writing a poem to Allius, but not for long. Just as the intrusive
picture of his brother, unknown and dead in Troy, briefly seizes
his mind at the beloved's advent, but passes to renewed joy at
that encounter, so the hold it has upon Catullus' poetical faculty
eases, and allows him to produce 68. The poet's love for Lesbia
is so strong that even in the midst of sorrow over fraternal loss
he can make poetry. It is poetry with his brother still at the center,
but nevertheless poetry of joyfulness and light. In an analogous
way, the love of the mistress, whom we may call Lesbia, is so
strong that the poet's brother is revivified through her.[2] Reborn

---

[1] See Luck, *The Latin Love Elegy* (page 30, note 6 above) 57 note 2.

[2] See page 49, note 1 below. Elder regards Lesbia as the object of
Catullus' love in 68.

in *68*, the brother's figure lives in the text as he did in the poet's mind on the wondrous occasion of Lesbia's coming to Catullus. Thus a tribute is made to the dead by acknowledging the power of a living woman.

In poem 68 the dead brother is at least as important as Lesbia. Apart from his privileged seat in the poem, he is endowed with a characteristic which only Lesbia approaches, namely, fulfilment. Except for the brother, and to a lesser extent Lesbia (and her *omnivolus* counterpart the god) all others in the poem suffer diminution, loss or retribution or are threatened by these. Allius is love-sick, though he is cured by the end of the poem. Catullus is beset by grief, though he too is assuaged. Laodamia is forever on the brink of being bereft of 'vita dulcius coniugium.' Paris will lose Helen. Hercules serves a *deterior erus*, and Hebe will lose her virginity. Even the unsympathetic legacy hunters are deprived of *gaudia*. Juno is dissatisfied with Jupiter's conduct. In the midst of bliss Catullus cites a drawback to his *mode de vivre* with Lesbia: Lesbia 'uno non est contenta Catullo' (135). Lesbia is in a position of strength. But only the brother, in death, is out of jeopardy, and his safety lies in his being beyond love. A flawed Lesbia lives in the *domus* which the poet has reconstituted with her, and there the brother has his place. Catullus, overcome with grief for his brother, recalls in *68* the concrete particularities of his love for Lesbia. He represents to himself, as well as to Allius and the world, the encounter with *candida diva* which refounded his *domus* once in time, and whenever the poet relives it in his mind. Both the brother and Lesbia are rehabilitated by *68*, which is the process of love tempering grief and giving life to the flawed living as well as to the dead.

Poem 68 is the most ambitious of all of Catullus' undertakings. In it he attempts to fill out an Alexandrian form with mythology which expresses his own personal feelings, as well as with an elevated statement of those feelings made *in propria persona*. The form in which these shifting themes of private joy and loss and public myth are set is a model of the poet's psychology. The form creates, or recreates, the mental process which the poet experiences and shapes. Virtually all of these techniques are new in literature, and remain unique in antiquity.[1] Catullus undertook a

---

[1] An exception may be seen in Propertius *4. 7*, which however is largely

good deal in *68*. The success of his venture is not to be measured
by the puzzlement and hostility of commentators who expect
rational discursiveness and are annoyed at finding something else.
Rather, Catullus' success or failure can be evaluated by the degree
of consistency exhibited by his polysemantic text when it is understood to represent psychological as well as objectively oriented
reality.

Poem 68 is unsurpassed as an honestly transcribed fragment
of a mental process which begs off a task because of grief, then
thaws and catches fire through recollection, and ends in joy as
great as the antecedent depression. Moreover, the joy does not
avoid the object causing depression but puts it in its place and
values it rationally. This poem also succeeds as a tightly organized
poetical structure, with exordium and conclusion in plain style,
and a carefully balanced main section. But as a series of images
developing an orderly grouping of thoughts and emotions, the
poem is an ostensible failure. It is perhaps not excessive nor irrelevant to call Allius' help a cool stream or a favorable breeze,
or opening up a field for loving. The comparison of the *domina*,
aflame with love, to Laodamia, about to lose her husband, superficially is inept. Likewise, the address to Nemesis seems out of
place, except as an involuted way of pointing out the poet's con-
viction of the rightness of his course with Lesbia. The intrusion
of Paris and Helen into a text which deals with the poet's love
for a married woman is in bad taste, from an objective point of
view, particularly since it is the irregular and destructive aspect
of the Trojan adventurer that is dwelt upon. The *barathrum* sequence
is particularly farfetched, seemingly introduced solely for the sake
of Hercules, whose presence in the text as a non-digressive figure
is unaccountable in terms of narrational surface and discursive
meaning. After the stoic saint, the old man, his late-born heir
and a pair of doves seem irrelevant even though they are points
of comparison to the *domina*. Furthermore, the conclusion does
not depict the disconsolate Allius and sad Catullus of the opening
section but men happy and secure.

These real objections have, it is hoped, been adequately answered
in the foregoing pages. A brief résumé may be in order. The relation-

---

an *admonitio*. Nevertheless Propertius' state of mind is of some moment.
It is Luck who draws attention to Catullus' uniqueness in *68*, (page 30, note
1 above) 53-54.

ship, *foedus amicitiae*, between Lesbia and Catullus, symbolically objectified by Laodamia, will suffer diminution through loss of a beloved. It will not be Catullus or an entire Lesbia, but the poet's brother (a part of Catullus), and a part of Lesbia. Laodamia is relevant as a figure signifying a joy which will end and a relationship which will not. Hercules is a relevant image setting forth the triumph of life in the midst of woe, and of the immortality which a man may win through generous actions. When these two figures are referred to the poet's psychological state, and when that mental state is not at rest but in motion, Laodamia and Hercules gain relevance. Laodamia is introduced as the depression nears its oppressive center. Hercules appears after the release of tension is achieved, and the poem and the poet pick up a rising course toward light and life. The continuing family and the natural passion of the doves are images consonant with this new outlook. The *domus* lost through the brother's death is re-integrated by loving Lesbia. As Catullus to some extent recognizes, his *foedus* with Lesbia is flawed, and the love which he bears for his dead brother is related to that defect in his love-relationship with his mistress. It may be that he rehabilitates Lesbia through his brother, whose love he transfers to her.[1] In view of this poem's movement, however, one may also say that it is the new *domus* with Lesbia that gives the brother a context in which he lives again. Lesbia has taught Catullus to redeem loss by love. Catullus will so teach Allius.[2]

Catullus risked failure with *68* but avoided it, at least with an ancient audience. It was only in modern times (as late as 1793) that the text was cut at line 40. As long as a rhetorical tradition, based on oral performance, was viable, the audience of a skilfull performer could hear for themselves the carefully controlled flowering of one of Catullus' most ambitious, least understood and yet generally successful poems. They could hear represented the slow blossoming from despair to joy that Catullus has here set down. In *68* he counsels Allius to live like a season, the *iucundum ver* (16) which is aware of death to follow, and is sensitive to betrayals. But Catullus the poet is conscious of joys inherent in some moments of time. 'quare illud satis est si nobis is datur unis/ quem

---

[1] Elder (page 1, note 1 above) 129 ff.
[2] See page 41, note 1 above.

lapide illa dies candidiore notat' (147 f.). He possesses a sure
knowledge of immortality derived from art: 'ne fugiens . . . aetas/
illius hoc caeca nocte tegat studium' (43 f.): 'ne vestrum scabra
tanget rubigine nomen/ haec atque illa dies atque alia atque
alia./ huc addent divi quam plurima . . .' (151 ff.). In *carmen* 68
he speaks to his friend, to Lesbia, to the world, but most of all
to himself.

In the practice of his art, Catullus relied in differing ways and
to various degrees upon his craft to identify, objectify and hence
communicate his artistic visions and intents. When a poem such
as *30* takes its place in the environment of the Catullan corpus,
it gains in implication by reference to other poems in a special
way. It is comprehensible without reference to the other poems,
but barely so. The other poems of Catullus do for the modern
critic what first-hand knowledge of the poet did for its recipient.
The meaning of the poem becomes clear because of context and
situation. This kind of poem, which looks outward to a circumstantial world, depends upon a language which normalizes experience, and hence can best be criticized by a method which
builds upon experience of the poet in other poems.

Poem 50 is different. In a relatively low-keyed situation it
replaces, for the poet, the emotion of strongly desiring to be with
his friend, and represents, for the recipient, the poet himself.
It itself constitutes a symbol for emotional frustration and release.
Accordingly, the best understanding of such an emotional
monument is along the lines of participation in the symbol, which
results in a closer view of the poet's values and preoccupations.
Poem 50 may be termed a static symbol of a recurring process.
The process is that of thinking about and cherishing the keeping
of faith.

Poem 65 demands a somewhat different critical approach.
Its order of words mirrors a psychological order without demanding
more of the audience than awareness of the poet's distress and of
the direction in which he will move to get relief. This poem is
continuous metaphor which occasions both form and sense. Both
shape and significance are distinguishable one from another,
even though one cannot be detached from the other. The complex
images of *65*, knitting together in a coherent whole, convey a
promise of life through rebirth. Poem 68 is that rebirth made art.

Poem 68 is the poet's mental process made accessible through the balancing of themes; structure and meaning have fused, and the poem signifies itself. All that is needed to understand it is to recognize it as movement and to gauge its pace. It is a dynamic revelation of a unique experience. The poem's text is coterminous with that experience. The text shapes that suffering and joy into meaning and art.

Through the art of poetry Catullus achieved a world by the ordering of words, and thereby gave life not only to others but to himself. Art was the means of illuminating and defining the emotional world in which as a poet he had talent to live. His mind strove toward an understanding of self, and at some point conceived of his interior life as art. His chief success is total reliance upon the world of the poem to become the metaphor of psychological inwardness, the poet's mind.

Printed in the United States
By Bookmasters